T0197036

Acclaim for ABIGAIL THOMAS's

Safekeeping

"This beguiling memoir reads like a novel, with characters one cares about and an engrossing and moving story."
—Hilma Wolitzer, author of *Wish You Were Here*

"Abigail Thomas has created magic for smart, curious readers. Her prose is poetic, charged with hope and promise. I admire every word she writes: her work makes me happy."   —Kaye Gibbons, author of *Ellen Foster* and *Charms for the Easy Life*

"Abigail Thomas wears her wisdom so lightly, so jauntily, that you barely notice a vision creeping up on you. Her memoir explores how women build selves out of scraps and shards—not just from love and happiness but from sorrow and failure too. Thomas has made a life for herself like a cook whipping up dinner from what's in the refrigerator. The result is a giddily satisfying feast."
—Lisa Zeidner, author of *Layover*

"An artful scatter of snapshot moments . . . revealing a life that's remarkable not for its events but for the way it's recalled, with rue, insight and wit."
—*Rocky Mountain News*

"Comprised of small, astonishing moments which have been strung together in a wholly fresh and gorgeous way . . . Consistently humble and beautiful . . . Thomas has given an honest shape to the fluidity of memory."
—*Bomb*

"*Safekeeping* sparkles like bits of a smashed mirror . . . Each is a moment reflected, and reflected upon. Peer into enough diamonds and shards and you see the story, you glimpse the soul. . . . Thomas also bears eloquent witness to her own life, as refracted by her keen eye and recorded in prose that verges on poetry."
—*Newsday*

"Precisely lyrical, silver-gilt, fevered, and in the end, sweet." —*Booklist*

"Reads like a collaboration between Richard Brautigan and Joni Mitchell . . . A refreshing testimonial for the unrepentant—and in Thomas's case unsinkable—youthful free spirit." —*The Austin Chronicle*

"Finally, a memoir in which sorrow and regret are part of a larger, more resounding joy. From bits and moments of her life—its quiet feminism, its loves and upheavals, mistakes, loyalties, adventures, and domesticities—Abigail Thomas offers up herself, most surprised by what is most familiar. To read *Safekeeping* is to be in it."
—Abby Frucht, author of *Life Before Death*

ABIGAIL THOMAS

Safekeeping

Abigail Thomas is the author of the novel *An Actual Life* and the story collections *Getting Over Tom* and *Herb's Pajamas*. She lives with her husband in New York City, where she teaches in the M.F.A. Writing program at the New School.

Safekeeping

Some True Stories from a Life

ABIGAIL THOMAS

ANCHOR BOOKS
A Division of Random House, Inc.
New York

FIRST ANCHOR BOOKS EDITION, APRIL 2001

Copyright © 2000 by Abigail Thomas

Grateful acknowledgment is made for permission to reprint an excerpt from "Something to Remember You By" by Howard Dietz and Arthur Schwartz. Copyright © 1930, copyright renewed by Warner Bros. Inc. Rights for extended renewal term in the United States controlled by Warner Bros. Inc. and Arthur Schwartz Music Ltd. Rights for the rest of the world controlled by Warner Bros. Inc. All rights reserved. Used by permission of Warner Bros. Publications U.S. Inc., Miami, FL 33014.

Thank you to *Double Take* (and especially David Rowell), *The Alaska Quarterly*, and *The East Hampton Star*, where some of these pieces originally appeared. And thanks to the MacDowell Colony, for the quiet to figure out what I was doing.

The Library of Congress has cataloged the Knopf edition as follows:
Thomas, Abigail.
Safekeeping : some true stories from a life /Abigail Thomas—1st ed.
p. cm.
ISBN 0-375-40807-X
1. Thomas, Abigail. I. Title.
HQ1058.5.U5 T48 2000
305.48'9654—dc21
[B] 99-040783
CIP

Anchor ISBN: 0-385-72055-6

Author photograph © Nancy Crampton

www.anchorbooks.com

For my family, again and again

Take a sad song and make it better.

—THE BEATLES, "Hey Jude"

PART ONE

Before

Before

Before I met you I played my music on a child's Victrola. I played *Music from Big Pink* over and over. "Tears of Rage." "The Weight." *Wheels of Fire*. I had three kids. We ate on the overturned kitchen drawer because I didn't have a table. I was young. I didn't know what things could happen. I spent my time in the moment; everything else was shoved ahead, like furniture I didn't need yet. We were crammed into a small space. My bed was in the living room.

I am remembering this time just before I knew you, and then I knew you, and then you died. It makes the parentheses within which I lived most of my life. Not knowing you, knowing you, and then you died. Twenty-seven years. A long time. You introduced my kids to a dining room table, you liked to joke proudly. Sometimes we sang songs. You were impressed. I knew the words to everything.

When we were together I remember my bedside book for years was *How to Stay Alive in the Woods*. "Anyone

Can Build a Lean-to," my favorite chapter. All you needed were two forked sticks and a pole. I studied the diagram and watched your face. I looked at the woods. They were right outside the door.

Offering

While you were alive the past was a live unfinished thing. Like a painting we weren't done with. Like a garden we were still learning to tend. Nothing was set in stone yet, and weren't we ourselves still changing? We might redeem our past by redeeming ourselves. I had in mind a sort of alchemy. But then you died, and just like that, it was over. What was done was done. Now we could never fix it. All I can do is chip away, see what comes off in my hand, look for a shape.

Something Valuable Given
Away on the Street

A middle-aged teacher is walking down Broadway in her
big white sneakers and her yellow socks, her too-long skirt
(stained where three drops of hair-tinting stuff fell on it);
she is wearing her daughter's jacket, a new red velvet
scarf, and her two haircuts, both bad, and she is thinking
about desire, that old plaything, whose provenance is no
longer detail but a vast inchoate longing. And so when the
man bearing the basket of freshly baked bread, round
loaves with cracked tops, some large, some small, gets out
of his truck and begins to walk toward the West Side
Market and their paths cross, she can't help saying, "God,
those look so beautiful." He smiles. He actually looks at
her. "Take one," he says. She says, "Oh no, I couldn't."
She almost bursts forth with I am just on my way to exer-
cise, otherwise I wouldn't look like this, in these shoes for
instance and no lipstick, with my bad hair and so forth, I
put on thirty pounds since I got married again . . . but she
holds her tongue. It isn't that sort of moment. Perhaps

there will never again be that sort of moment, and that is okay with her. Instead she pauses, looking at the loaves. "Go ahead," he urges her again, holding the basket out to her, smiling. She smiles back.

"Really?" She chooses a small round loaf.

"Portuguese bread," he tells her, "very good."

"Thank you," she says, stuffing it into her purple plastic bag on top of her gym clothes and her copy of *Winesburg, Ohio*. As she walks away she feels not young again, perish the thought, but oh so glad to be alive, and middle-aged, and female, and walking down Broadway. She is not wishing he had invited her back to his bakery to bed her later among the bowls of flour and yeast. She is not regretting the loss of youth. She does not want more than the bread he gave her and the moment on the sidewalk. Does this mean she has finally grown up? And what was this new feeling but a sort of all-purpose longing which does not need to be satisfied but rather must be renewed each day on the streets of her city? I live in a perpetual state of desire, she realizes. Things could be worse.

She gets to her gym and assumes her position on a treadmill in the window, which nobody ever looks up at. She is on treadmill number 8, her favorite, because of the handlebars. She nods in friendly fashion to the women on treadmill numbers 7 and 9. One of them is the one with the Frida Kahlo eyebrows. It is a women's gym. We are all middle-aged, she thinks merrily, treading away at 3.9 miles per hour. The only eyes that meet ours on the street are one another's. Except her husband who sometimes walks by and salutes her on his way to his aged mother. And the occasional baker. She has slung her purple bag over the treadmill handlebars and can see the bread in there. Life is so sweet, she thinks, her brain taking up the rhythm of her stride, one two three FOUR, five six seven EIGHT, one two three FOUR, five six seven EIGHT.

She will have to tell her class. Make up an assignment. Write two pages in which something valuable is given away on the street. What will they come up with, she wonders, wanting to know.

Apple Cake

I am not a girl. I am the grandmother of six. I bake cakes for all my grandchildren. My name is synonymous with "cake." I have taught them this. Nana, Cake, and they clap their little hands. Apple cake, this is my specialty. In the past twelve days I have baked seven apple cakes for seven separate occasions. These cakes contain walnuts and raisins as well as golden oil and apples. You would beg me for a slice if you could see these cakes. You would beg for their perfume alone. They do well for holidays. Thanksgiving, for example. Anniversaries.

I have had my good times and my bad. This was long ago, my dears, before most of you were born. I was not a prudish girl. Nor was I wise. When I was young I gave myself away; it was all I had to offer. But not today. Today I will bake a cake. The cake is not a metaphor. Say the words "apple cake." Apple cake.

See how the mouth fills with desire.

What a Waste

She was not always a teacher. She was a girl once, a girl who married and married again, hoping to find happiness for both herself and her children. It was as simple as that, although she herself was complicated, as were her husbands, not to mention her kids. Her second husband didn't know what he wanted in a wife. No doubt that was why he had never married. Still a bachelor at forty-six. Oh so eligible. "Are you pregnant?" one of his old friends asked her rudely. "How did you get him to marry you?" She wanted to be witty but wasn't. The woman was fat and she leaned against a beautifully curved banister. That's all she remembers from that party, at which she got drunk.

Her new husband thought it was funny and dismissed it with a wave. "What do you care?" he asked her, winking at his old friend across the room. He had many sophisticated old friends and all she had were her kids and some ragtag-and-bobtails from the Village. It would have been easier if only he had said he loved her, but instead he was scientific. Love, he would say, what is it? A word. Later she found out that he thought it gave a woman the upper hand if you told her you loved her.

Invent a New Creation Myth

Her old friend, formerly her second husband, is sick in bed. She has brought him lunch. Once upon a time when they were married he was always upset. With her housekeeping. With her cooking. There is no marmalade on this table, he might well have said. But now they are friends, and he loves her to bring him food. "When did you become such a good cook?" he wants to know. She no longer reminds him that she was always a good cook. She smiles instead. "Eat," she says. Around his place at the table there is always a little circle of spilled food. Rice, peas. She watches him now sitting on pillows, eating in the sunlight, talking to her, happy, and now and then crumbs fly out of his mouth, small particles borne on his breath, his excited talk. Maybe this was how the universe was created, she thinks. A deity at breakfast, talking with his mouth full, and the crumbs shooting forth became the stars and galaxies. She laughs but doesn't tell him the thought. Am I making a mess? he might ask her. She wants him to keep eating. She wants him to get well.

Spelling It Out

There are already a lot of husbands floating around, my sister says.

Well yes, I say. I married three times.

That's what I'm saying. A lot of husbands. Somebody's going to get confused. Maybe even annoyed.

Well then I'll spell it out. I got pregnant when I was eighteen. I got married. My husband was a student. We had three kids, but I left after eight years.

That's one, says my sister. That brings us to 1968.

Then I went back to New York City with my kids and after two years I got married again. He was a physicist and we moved to the suburbs. We had one child. Then we got divorced.

That's two, says my sister. Now it's 1978.

Then I moved back to New York City and after eleven years I married again, this time a reporter. We're still married.

That's three, says my sister. Now what was so hard about that? she asks.

Good Manners

"I'm going to have a baby," I told them. My boyfriend and I were holding hands on the brown couch in my parents' living room. "I'm really sorry," I added. I was eighteen. It was 1960. My father and mother were understandably upset, but they got hold of themselves. "We will make it all right," my father said.

Soon I was married. Everyone had good manners; that was how we got through it. Sometimes the four of us sat in my mother and father's living room and they asked my new husband, nineteen years old, about school and politics and what books he'd read and listened politely when he answered. It was civilized. Once a friend of my young husband's came to the door and after meeting my mother pronounced her a real babe. When I told her, I thought it would please her, but I was wrong.

Thirty years later, long after we had been divorced, our three children grown, my father lay dying and my first husband asked if he could come to pay his respects. "Yes," I said, "of course." I wondered what he would say. They hadn't seen each other more than half a dozen times in many years. I wondered what he would say; what could he say? I stood outside the hospital room, and although I didn't want to intrude, I heard my former husband speak.

"I've come to wish you well," he said.

Unfamiliar

So there we were, my husband and I, up for the weekend at my parents' new apartment where soot gathered quickly on the windowsills and the hall smelled funny. My parents had moved. We were on our best behavior— napkins in our laps, speaking when spoken to, laughing at jokes, feigning interest in the news. Then it got late, and my husband and I were lying in bed with the lights out when my father came in unannounced. He didn't knock. He was in a very good mood; he had that excited happy tone in his voice. He wanted to tell us something, or per- haps read us a scrap of something interesting from the paper. It was past midnight. He flipped on the lamp. We lay there politely, and after a while he left, the smell of whiskey in the air. Good night, he cried happily, good night you two. Suddenly my husband sat up in bed. He was wearing pajamas. He was in a furious rage. Your fa- ther has no respect for me, he said. I said in a small voice, What do you mean? He said, To have just come barging in like that. He wanted me to tell my father how rude he had been. He was nineteen. I felt bad. My poor father. It was my fault, everything. The light was still on.

That night the baby kicked so it wasn't a complete wash.

Visiting Nurse

My baby and I ate scrambled eggs and creamed spinach every night for several weeks. We both liked this meal. She was my first baby and I was young. My husband was at the library studying, and my baby and I sat at the kitchen counter in our tiny apartment. Our parents paid the rent. We were living near the college where my husband was finishing his sophomore year. The super came up and told me not to leave Brillo on the radiator as it was bad for children. My child is not going to stuff a Brillo pad into her mouth, I didn't reply. Instead I thanked him humbly. Everybody knew more than I did. Everyone had advice. Bananas are good for babies, the visiting nurse said. Potassium. And it will bind the bowels a bit. My child and I had had problems in the loose-bowel department, too much creamed spinach, too many scrambled eggs, too many nights in a row.

My child had gotten hot, too, a fever, and this was why I called the visiting nurse who came and put the baby right away in a tub of ice-cold water. She didn't look twice at our unmade bed, the books piled on the floor. My baby screamed and screamed, but the nurse explained what she was doing and what I should do next time. The nurse was not scornful of me and she didn't condescend. I stood in the doorway with my hands clasped tight behind my back, concentrating on what I needed to know.

Young Wasn't It

You weren't young, my sister says. You have to explain it better.

What do you mean, I say. You think eighteen is mature?

Unprepared, she says. You were unprepared. Why?

Because I was young, I insist.

No. That's not it. Were we told to wear our scarves?

That was for sissies, I say. We didn't care about those things.

Did we care about wet feet or chapped hands?

Certainly not.

Mom didn't exactly spend her days in a red-checked apron plying us with little goodies, now did she.

Well, why would she? I ask. That didn't float her boat.

Au contraire, says my sister. It torpedoed her boat. She wasn't born to put on our little mittens and then hang them up to dry.

No, but we knew where Ovid was buried, didn't we?

Banished, she says. Where Ovid was banished.
Right. Banished. Where was it again?
Some island, she says.

An Issue of Clothes

We had a laundry chute. You opened a little door and threw things. They slid down, and they ended up in a basket in the basement, but from there they didn't go anywhere. It was a dead end. Nobody in the family knew how to do laundry. Pretty soon you were out of clothes. We don't recall our mother doing laundry. Once a week she counted handkerchiefs and socks and sent them out. I remember this made her very mad. She stood there in the hall with an angry look and counted noisily, ticking things off on a list. We didn't disturb her. It all seemed very mysterious. So finally it seemed wiser to hang on to your clothes and keep wearing them even if they got dirty.

We think she never learned how to do laundry because where she grew up laundry just got done. For a while our mother employed a Russian woman named Mrs. Gregorette. Mrs. Gregorette loved to iron. She took a mouthful of water from a glass she kept on the counter and then sprayed it on the clothes. Right out of her

mouth! My mother enjoyed this very much, and our hor-
ror. Laundry was not what our mother concentrated on.
She concentrated on our father. They were very much in
love.

Watching Her Father Eat Cake

I remember making cakes when I got home from school. They were always yellow, as I didn't know how to separate an egg, and always from mixes, but they were thrilling to make. I looked forward to it all day and rushed home from school. I can still remember the silky feel of the cellophane bag that held the yellow powder and cracking the eggs one by one on the side of the bowl. I usually ate so much batter that the cakes were very small. The icing was made out of confectioners' sugar and butter and milk, and I melted bitter chocolate and poured it on top of the whole thing, my grandmother's recipe. My father sometimes had two pieces. "This is very good cake," he told me. "How did you make such a good cake?" and I would explain it to him. He was an important man, a scientist who often stayed at his lab till all hours. It made me shy to have his full attention, but I watched carefully as he ate every bite, his jaw clicking now and then as he chewed.

Jimi

A familiar sound is coming from behind her grandsons' closed door. The walls shake. Her grandsons are into Jimi Hendrix and she thinks she will buy them a poster. She remembers Jimi from the old days, how sexy he was, how wicked. A kind of god, really. She can swoon even today with the memory. "Are You Experienced," she finds herself whispering as she walks into a store. Imagine her surprise when she looks at the poster. What she sees is not someone she would take home to bed but take home to feed. He is so skinny. So young. She would make him chicken and dumplings today, and her apple cake. She would give him her pot roast and vegetables. Eat, she would say, eat.

I Ran Away

I ran away from my first husband. Often we fought, and when we weren't fighting we were polite. "Excuse me," we would say if our feet touched under the table, like strangers in a restaurant. We were children, not meant to be married, but we did make beautiful babies. I ran four hundred miles away and lived in my parents' basement. They had a house in New York City. I was twenty-six with three children. We all threw up our hard-boiled eggs on the airplane. My middle daughter brought her dee-dee, a pink fuzzy bathrobe that was her companion. The children's ages were seven, five, and three. My parents welcomed us, but their hearts must have been filled with fear. How will she live? When will she leave? I imagined them whispering at night. At the end of every day my mother would collect our scattered belongings and lay them at the top of the stairs to the basement in hopes I would get organized. After a few months I got a job. I made $56.90 a week.

The children were still small. Good things might still happen. We might all live happily ever after if only I could find the right man.

Everyone Agreed

It was 1968, but she was a child of the fifties, she needed a man. And not just any man, a husband. A husband would provide her with a center. She had none of her own. Her parents too wanted her to marry again. After a suitable interval. After a quiet time, as her mother once put it. Her parents were happily married. Didn't her mother still take her glasses off to dance with her father? Didn't they still kiss with their eyes closed? Marriage was safer than being at large.

Not Just for Myself

I was looking for a father for my kids. I was not in it just for myself. Would you make a good father? I would wonder no matter who it was, no matter if we'd met five minutes before. No matter if he drove a truck or sold loose joints. They would have been amazed if they'd known what I was thinking. Of course it wasn't the only thing I was thinking. A lot of the time I wasn't thinking at all. I slept with many men. One was paralyzed and we made love on the living room rug in my parents' apartment. They were in Washington, and my children were all asleep. I can't recall his name. We took off his leg braces and laid them to one side. He'd had polio when he was little. They invented the vaccine six months after he got sick. He would have made a good father to my children, I thought. But he never called me up, and he lived in North Carolina anyway. After a few days I slept with somebody else. He worked in an office. He was much older than I was, and he was married, but he kissed me in the mail room and he said my lips were soft. After that we took his motorcycle every Wednesday and ate French fries and hot pastrami. We drank celery soda. Then we went to a cheap hotel. I still remember the old yellow blinds.

It was this same man who gave me a plastic blow-up banana, six feet tall. That was to make up for the fact that he stood me up one night he'd been going to come over. I waited downstairs on the stoop for hours. I didn't know what else to do. I already had the babysitter. I wasn't too bright in those days. Up yours, I hadn't learned to say. Besides, he was a genuinely nice man. He sent me to the dentist and paid for it. He sewed the buttons on my coat himself, with skill. I never called him by his first name, not even in bed. I put the banana in the living room and after a few weeks I let the air out and threw it away. It took up too much space. The kids were disappointed.

Respect for My Elders

I had respect for my elders, which was why I never called him by his first name. He was a friend of my boss. Mr. Gladstone, how's about a blow job? No. I never said such things. I didn't have to. We all know certain things intuitively, such as when a man smiles at you and pushes your head in the general direction of his crotch. I thought it was romantic because of the absence of words. I felt sophisticated, experienced. I don't mean to sound bitter. I'm not bitter. I am only a little bit amused, looking back, this view from the person I have finally become. Now if I thought my daughters were calling anybody Mr. Anything in bed, then you'd see the fur fly. "I'm all out of estrogen, but I do have a gun." I heard that from my friend Tracy. But bitter? Not me.

Inappropriately Dressed for the Occasion

The music was still playing, and here and there drunks were asleep on the furniture, but she found herself in a dwindling group. Where was everybody? Her friend appeared at her elbow. Come into the bedroom, he said, that's where everybody is. She was awfully drunk. Not stoned, she hated marijuana. It was 1968.

There were a whole bunch of people on the bed and clothes all over the floor. She had only heard about orgies, never been to one. But I'm wearing my new dress, she protested to no one in particular. She did look awfully good in it; it was brown and clung to every part of her and it was short as was fashionable. Come on, said a friend, beckoning. How young he looked without his clothes on. He was smiling. She put out her cigarette. The Doors were on, or was it Cream? The music was wonderfully loud. *I'd like to have another kiss.* Oh me too, she must have thought. Who wouldn't.

It was hard to know where to climb aboard so to speak. There were so many bodies already on the bed. It was like being part of some coral reef, only soft, with many moving parts. You couldn't tell where you ended and the others began. It wasn't sexy at all, not really, it was something else she can't explain. Good-natured, maybe. And she kept her dress on. But here it is thirty years later, and sometimes she misses it, whatever it was.

No Underwear

I can't explain it, I say.

My sister says, There were shops. You could have bought some.

I can't explain it, I say again. I didn't wear any. I wasn't happy about it. It's just the way it was.

Why, why, why, asks my sister. How could you have gone out into the street in a miniskirt?

How could I have done it? It gave me a focus. Instead of thinking about how I had no education and no job experience and couldn't type and had no husband and three kids and no future that I could even begin to imagine, instead of that I could focus on Jeez here I am with no underwear again. Better stand up straight.

I don't think that's it, says my sister.

Maybe I just wanted the attention, like a six-year-old who knocks the lamp off the table while his folks read the paper. Very childish. I agree completely. How about that? Does that hold water?

My sister shakes her head. No, she says, but her voice is patient. What do they want, she asks, those young girls who are so promiscuous?

I don't know, I say.

Yes you do, says my sister. What are they looking for?

I don't know, I say.

Yes you do, says my sister.

Love? I ask.

Right, says my sister. That's right.

Looking for love in all the wrong spaces? I say, laughing.

And that's all they think they have to offer, says my sister. You have to say that.

But of course, I say. That's so obvious.

Well you have to write it, says my sister.

Okay, I say. I will. I went around with no underpants. It was like a big advertisement. Here. This is all I have to offer. Check it out. And everyone who showed any interest I followed home. There. Are you satisfied now?

Exhausted

She was always tired then. That is why being tired now makes her feel young. She was up all day and half the night what with the kids and the boyfriends. What with the cigarettes and the whiskey. What with the wild wild women. (She was the wild wild woman herself of course.) Got no sleep. Didn't really care. Still looked good. Loved her kids. Once she hitched a ride home at three in the morning from Avenue C. She was waiting for the bus, and a couple of guys stopped; she could see through the car windows they had martini glasses in their hands. One of them rolled his window down and started to hit on her a little bit. "Lookin' good," he probably said, or "Big legs," one of the compliments of those days. It was four degrees above zero and she was wearing loafers with no socks and no stockings and her coat had only one button left. She wasn't much of a dresser. The driver said, she could hear through the window, "Leave her alone, man, it's too cold. Don't hassle the chick." She said, "Can I have a ride to Fifth?" and they opened the back door. They were friendly and very nice. She knew it would be okay. And it was okay. They let her out on the corner of Fifth Avenue and Eighth Street where she lived. She was sure she knew what was safe and what wasn't. And luckily for her, she was right most of the time. The rest of the time she was lucky.

Those days are gone forever and good riddance no doubt. What is it, thirty years ago? The world seemed innocent then. She knows now it wasn't. She looks at her watch. Two-thirty in the morning. She is tired, but nothing is wasted, she uses it to remember the old days. Exhaustion is her servant, where once it was her master. She looks out her window, uptown, at the water towers, at the squares of light in other windows. Where a man she hadn't met back then, a man she was about to meet, a man whom she would love and hate and love again, a man with whom she would spend the next thirty years, give or take, has died. Died. It seems impossible. She can almost see his windows from her window. She can almost hear his voice. Anything might happen. She doesn't want to go to bed.

A Simple Solution

At suppertime I pulled out the bottom drawer in the kitchen cupboard and turned it upside down because we didn't have a table. Then we sat on the floor and ate off it. I felt resourceful. We had moved out of my parents' house into our own apartment. The rent was cheap. You could live on nothing in 1969. I made $90 a week, but my monthly rent was only $143.35. We lived on West Twelfth Street between Sixth and Seventh. It was a nice neighborhood, St. Vincent's across the street. We made do with what we scrounged up.

My middle daughter complains of those days, but something else bothered her. When they were all three in the tub, she and her sister and her brother, she says, I would put in my dirty feet, stuck all over with raisins and soot and god knows what all. I went barefoot and it was New York City. She says I did this over her protests night after night. I did not, I want to say, but I think she's right. It rings a bell. I didn't understand what was so bad.

Perhaps I wanted to be one of the kids instead of the mother. Forgive me. There are so many things I would never do again.

"Hey Jude"

Sometimes she goes back downtown where she lived so long ago, and she walks through the park at Washington Square. She was barefoot here all summer in 1968 and 1969, her feet tough as hooves. She was slender and foolish and skimpily clad. She sat on the rim of the fountain, and her three young children splashed with all the other children in the water. It was a place so full of life and what seemed like hope back then, and possibility, and adventure. The Vietnam War was on, and they all believed so earnestly that things must and could change, a single voice raised with other voices would fix the world. And making love was really making love, they thought, something hopeful was released into the air, every time, like a nutrient for the planet. She craved experience and she confused experience with sex. Not to knock it. But it isn't the be-all and end-all she'd once thought.

Despite the exhilaration, it was not a good time. Along with the excitement was always the fear, running by her side. She didn't know what would become of her and her three children. Because what was she doing? She was like the eye of a hurricane, high wind and water all around. She would (if she could) put her arm around the girl she'd been and try to tell her Take it easy, but the girl would not have listened. The girl had no receptors for Take it easy. And besides, "Hey Jude" was on the radio, it was her prayer, her manifesto, almost her dwelling place. She sang it everywhere. The music made her cry then; it makes her cry now. Listening to it now brings back memories so sharp they taste like blood in her mouth.

She walks back along Eighth Street toward her subway. It's cold, and she is wearing warm clothes and boots, and a coat that fits and has all its buttons. Her children are grown now, with good lives of their own. She pauses, waiting for the light. For some reason the old Whelan's on the corner of Sixth Avenue and Eighth Street occupies a soft spot in her memory. It is gone now, that dreadful place with a lunch counter where twenty-four hours a day people sat slumped over cups of bad coffee and at four in the morning you could buy cigarettes and Binaca. She wouldn't return to those days. But she can cry over them. As if youth were a limb that had tormented her, and its phantom remains, and she can still feel it aching, and she misses it because it was her own.

Mumps and My
Second Husband

I remember you called me up. You had been given my name by an old friend. You asked if I would like to go out for a drink sometime. I was busy and distracted. I forgot you were a physicist, that I would have nothing to say to you. "Have you had mumps?" I asked, a dish towel over my shoulder, a cigarette in my left hand. "My children have the mumps." You asked your mother. She was still living in the same apartment she had occupied for forty years. You called your childhood pediatrician, but he was dead. Your aunt remembered though. "I've had mumps," you called later to say. "Okay then," I said, no inkling that we would know each other until the day you died. "Come over." My children were already better. My sister would babysit.

He Filled My Door

He filled my door. He wore a winter coat that hadn't come off a thrift-shop rack. He was tall. He had a presence, as they say. And he looked familiar. There are the ones you recognize, after all. Oh, I thought. There you are. He came in to meet my children. He sat down on the white rocker for a few minutes, then he got up. He had come to take me out to dinner. I knew he liked the looks of me. I liked the looks of him. He had nice hands. He had big shoulders. He had a wonderful wicked smile. What did we talk about? Maybe he told me then he had grown up on Washington Square in a brownstone with a Tiffany ceiling. That when he was a little boy he had crawled out over the ceiling on a grid that allowed you to replace the bulbs. He had done this quite often, although he had been forbidden, shorting out all the fuses in the house. His father, incensed, would try to catch him, but if he could make it to the dining room table, his father could never catch him. He could run around it faster and finally his father gave up. His father was a doctor with two sets of patients, the rich ones whom he charged and the poor whom he did not. There were separate entrances. At this point I may have told him my son had cut the cords to a couple of lamps in my mother's living room. We had heard popping sounds, tiny explosions, and running into the room we found him under a table with the scissors in his hand. He was four. He liked the noise and the sparks. But maybe my mind is putting these together now. Anyway, we went somewhere in his green Mustang and afterward he said he'd like to see me again. We barely grazed mouths, but the air was electric.

He was very attractive; even my sister thought so. I liked him. I believed it when he said he'd call me again, although my sister was skeptical. But he knew what he wanted and he went after it. I understood that in the first five minutes. I felt strong suddenly. I was twenty-seven and he was forty-six. I had three children and he had never been married. I thought I knew what I needed to know. He thought he knew everything. He was my knight in shining armor come to save me. From what? From myself.

Nine months later we were married. We made each other laugh. What could go wrong?

Something Overheard

It was at a party in what was to become SoHo, lots of drinking, lots of smoke, and somebody said something I didn't catch, and another man replied, one hand on the back of his own head, the other holding a cigarette, both men wearing togas as I recall, "Oh honey, *any* sense of security is a false sense of security." Everybody laughed, but I didn't get it. I just didn't get it. What was so funny? What did it mean?

Now I get it.

In the Morning

The first night I slept at your apartment I thought you had
two dogs, both of them barking at me. It turned out there
was only one. I never liked your dog. She ate a hole in my
best skirt, the only truly expensive thing I had ever bought
myself. She dragged it off the chair where I'd thrown it.
Look at my skirt! I cried. Buy another, you said laughing,
handing me some money. But it was one of a kind, I said,
I can't buy another, but you didn't hear. You were happy.
You couldn't fathom skirt = damage. I did take the money
though. Fifty dollars was a lot in 1969.

The Money

My sister is upset about the money.

How much did he give you? Fifty dollars? Did you ask for that much?

It's what the skirt cost, I tell her. You remember that skirt. It was handmade. I got it on Greenwich Avenue. It was the one you said made my ass look like two basketballs bouncing up and down when I walked.

I remember it now.

Ha-ha, I say.

Didn't you feel funny taking it? she asks.

What. The money? Sort of, yes, I say.

Why did it make you feel funny? she repeats, her eyes fixed on my face.

I don't know, I say. It just did.

Because it was like payment?

I look at her, astonished. Of course not, I say.

Are you sure? You spent the night with this man and he gives you fifty bucks in the morning.

The dog ate my skirt, I say. Or did you forget that little fact.

I'm just asking why you felt funny, that's all. Don't get so hot under the collar.

It's because money was not the answer. *I'm sorry* was the answer.

My sister nods vigorously. *Bad dog* was the answer.

Damn right. Bad dog. But I took the money.

A Proposal of Marriage

After nine months I asked what his intentions were. "I can't keep leaving my children like this," I said, "every weekend." I had had a few swigs from the Vandermint chocolate liqueur bottle that he kept on the marble sideboard. Every time I walked past I took another delicious swallow. It wasn't like liquor. It was like candy with attitude. "I think I'm probably going to marry you," he said. He was sitting at his kitchen table. Why did this frighten me? What did I know? "Oh my god," I probably said, "thank you." I was desperately young. I'm certain we kissed.

But maybe not. Maybe I said, "Oh really? Have you thought about asking me first?" This is perfectly possible. At twenty-seven I had a certain moxie that passed for pride. But my memory fails me. I know he was a handsome man. Later, "Dance for me while the chicken is cooking," he suggested, sitting back on the sofa, his hands behind his head, feet on the coffee table. That I remember clearly.

But I married him anyway.

You Felt What You Felt

Before they got married he bought a house for all of them to live in. For her and her three children, and the child they planned to have together. It was an old house that overlooked the Hudson River. It sat high on a hill next to some woods. This seemed like a good idea. They needed lots of room. He had never been married before and never lived with children. There were five bedrooms and four bathrooms and three floors. There were three fireplaces. Was she a princess in a fairy tale? Was she as happy as she was supposed to be? She kept worrying about this.

When the kids had gone to school and her husband to work, she would sometimes sit in the living room holding tightly to the arms of the chair feeling afraid and think, Maybe it is the woodwork getting me down. The woodwork was dark and chin high around all the rooms. Then she got pregnant and for a little while knew who she was again. When the child was born, everyone loved her. But all was not well. She wanted to live happily ever after, but that was an awful responsibility. Her children were sup-

posed to live happily ever after now too and they weren't doing that either. What she had done in a small apartment seemed harder on this giant screen. And there she was, tiny in the corner. She didn't know that you weren't supposed to feel anything. You felt what you felt.

The Stanhope

Being no dummy, her second husband had introduced himself to her parents by taking them to the Stanhope for lunch. They liked him immediately. He knew art, which put him in good with her mother, and he was a scientist, which gave him lots in common with her father. He showed himself to be witty and happy, he was successful and interesting, he was handsome and solvent and in love with their daughter. She didn't even have to talk. Her mother and father looked at each other and smiled when lunch was over. Everything would be all right; she could feel their relief. They could stop worrying. After lunch they could stroll across the street to the Met and look at Caillebotte. She felt proud to have bagged such a big fish.

We Had a Daughter

We had a daughter together. You loved her. You were in the delivery room when she was born, something un-heard of, undreamed of, when my first three babies came. You held her in your arms when she was minutes old. I was happy. You were the man to share my children with, a father ready to be a father. My three children loved the baby too, although my son had hoped for a baby brother. There is a snapshot of my oldest daughter, then twelve, holding tight to the baby, as if she didn't want to give her back.

Definition of "Marriage"

My mother said to me, "Your father likes to think he is personally responsible for the sunrise. He thinks that if he didn't stand in front of the window every morning and supervise, the sun would never come up. What he doesn't know," she went on to say, "is that he couldn't do any of it if I didn't get up first and make the coffee and open the curtains."

For the longest time that was the definition of "marriage" for me.

I Found Out Later

My second husband wanted to mold me. Those were his very words. How I found out was he told somebody who told my sister who then told me. This was years later, of course. Way after. It was yesterday, in fact, as my sister and I were sitting at a table drinking expensive coffee cooked by furious youths. "He planned to *mold* you," my sister repeated, shaking her head in disbelief. "And this a man with a Ph.D.? And you say *you* were uneducated?"

It didn't work out. He wanted a woman who could set the table without once forgetting what kind of spoon he ate his cereal with. Forgetting the right spoon he interpreted as anger, and he couldn't enjoy food served by an angry person. Pretty soon I began leaving off the forks as well. So I can understand his complaints up to a point. But if the brisket did get cooked, and if it was melt-in-the-mouth tender, and the carrots and potatoes were perfect and distinct, and he couldn't quite tell—what did you put in the sauce that gives it the piquancy? (the answer is cinnamon, but I never told)—in other words if the food was good, I don't see that he should have held her mood against the cook. If she had more than one, which of course she did.

Neither does my sister.

Fencing

For him love/marriage was a fencing match; you never allowed your opponent the upper hand. Your mate was your opponent, although it was all in good fun. You never revealed your vulnerable spot, but you went after theirs with the lightest of touches. Touché, you might whisper under your breath, proud of your ability to remind but not wound. Touché. But you kept a certain distance. This did not of course preclude love. Love was most definitely part of this. It made the game so much more interesting. You laughed, you lunged and parried, you were nimble on your feet, you aimed not to hurt but only to touch lightly some sensitive place and then back off with a smile. I always loved talking to you, he told me later, even at our worst I always loved talking to you.

Me too, I said. Me too.

An Artist of Sorts

One year he took a sabbatical to paint. Physics was put away for a while. He made something out of everything. He made cats out of oaktag with pennies glued on for feet. They stood up sturdily and he was proud of them. He twisted birds out of scraps of wire. He made profiles out of Styrofoam, a head with a small cigar clenched in its mouth, a button for an eye, and shreds of god knew what glued on for hair. He made dogs and birds and faces. He was as interested in the packing materials of an object as in the object itself. He painted flowers. He once painstakingly cut a hand out of thick brass. His own, of course. "Dog Contemplating the Universe" was the caption of one of his favorite drawings. It was a brown dog, gazing blankly up at the moon. He wrote poems and stories. He made rhymes. "Rise and shine, rise and shine, you've had your sleep and I've had mine" heralded the start of a good day. "We only live once, if at all," one of his favorite sayings. It took me twenty years to find that funny.

His Suggestion

One time, when they were first married and he was still interested, he suggested she might want to wear a padded bra. He said it would look good on her, that her body was really made for a bigger bust, the proportions would look nice. She agreed. She appreciated that he had an opinion about what she was wearing, how she looked. He was much older than she and had a lot of experience with women, many of them quite well dressed.

But she felt very funny putting it on the first time. What am I doing? she wondered, adjusting the straps, looking this way and that in the mirror.

Nothing Was Anywhere

Her three kids sat around the wooden table in the kitchen. She was cooking supper, the baby cooing on the counter in her infant seat. Everything was everywhere. Potato peels, eggshells in the sink. Her husband came in and it made her jumpy. He hated a mess. He opened a drawer, then banged it shut. "Where do you keep the can opener?" he asked. The truth was she didn't keep the can opener anywhere. The can opener was wherever she'd last left it; the can opener was where she found it. Sometimes it was in the drawer. "What do you need it for?" she asked. "I'll do it." He shook his head. "Never mind."

"Can opener, can opener," she half sang as if nothing were wrong. "You have no system," he said wearily, picking up a magazine and watching a piece of paper flutter to the floor. She stooped for the paper and then rifled around in the sink. There it was, under the cake pan. "Here," she said, wiping it off on her apron. He didn't say anything. He opened a bottle of raspberry fruit drink and left the can opener on the counter. She was by now back at the stove humming in a casual fashion. But her face fell in spite of herself. Later, with a mouth full of home fries, one of the kids asked, "Mom? Are you happy?" "Goddamn it!" she shouted. "I am very happy!"

Chaos

Of course housekeeping was only the ostensible reason. The truth is it alarmed him to have to stick with just one woman. Here was a man who appreciated them all. Just one? he must have thought to himself. For the rest of my life, just this one? Such limitation smacked of mortality. And of course there were her kids. They made noises and demands. They were apt to misplace his Scotch tape. They finished all the milk. The household he lived in now was so chaotic. Chaos also meant death. He needed control of his habitat.

Not that they hadn't had hopes. There were wild grapes in the backyard of the house he bought and she planned to make jelly or something out of them and he thought about wine. Then they had stood together with their arms around each other, surveying the hilly yard. "Look at that tree," he'd said with wonder. "That's my tree. I could even cut it down if I wanted to." Later he built her a special platform so she could knead her bread more comfortably, with no strain on her back. She loved to bake, and he loved her anadama bread. His eyes would close when he put a piece in his mouth and stay closed while he ate. They had a big window installed in the kitchen that looked into the woods. In the fall afternoons she used to watch them empty of their light like a glass of bourbon slowly being filled to the brim.

Nothing under Her Hood

She wasn't like a car. You couldn't open her hood and tinker around. Besides, there wouldn't have been anything under her hood. Just empty space. She was afraid that there was no herself, that somehow she had gotten into this body, but she was too small for it, tiny. She was fooling people who thought she was real, and here. Her husband used to say, "But we are all nothing. None of us is anything at all." But she didn't know what he meant by that.

Overturned Rowboat

When she was very upset ("very upset" was how she put it to herself) and didn't know why yet, she went to her father. She couldn't help herself. This was toward the end of her second marriage. They sat out back on an overturned rowboat. She stared at the gray paint peeling off the boat and the grass growing up alongside. She told him she was scared all the time and that it scared her that she was scared. She said she got dizzy in the mornings. She said she was afraid to drive. Her father listened; she didn't recall his ever listening so carefully before. He called her dearie-pie. He patted her hand. This was so unexpected that it made her not recognize herself. It made her feel good, but it took her outside herself, as if the real her were sitting at the other end of the boat, watching. What does a grown woman do when her father pats her hand? How does she respond? She wanted him to know his gesture was welcome but at the same time it didn't fix anything. She tried to remember if he had ever patted her hand before. She didn't want to hurt his feelings, he was being so kind. But she was not okay. How should she act? She kept watching herself from the stern of the boat. This made her all the more scared. Because what if she was going crazy?

Then What Did He Say?

What did he say, my sister asks, after he patted your hand?

He said he wanted to help.

But what else did he say?

He asked me about my fevers.

And?

He asked about my dizzy spells and my headaches. And he made me a doctor's appointment. Someone he knew.

A shrink?

Are you kidding? No. That would have scared me to death. A regular doctor.

Then what?

I went to him and there was nothing wrong with me.

His Affair

My husband's affair (I found out later) was with a woman who put many different kinds of sausages and wild birds and pigs into a big pot and cooked them with garlic. It was delicious but frightening. We were at her New Year's Eve party. She seemed very sophisticated. I had never heard of and could not spell the names of her sausages and she wasn't interested in giving me the recipe anyway, certainly not in the middle of the huge party she was throwing. All she told me was that it took three days to prepare and it was called hunter's stew and was an old family recipe. She was a heavy-breasted woman; she wore feathers and shawls and I seem to remember some beautiful and exotic jewelry and combs in her swept-up hair, but perhaps my mind has embellished her. I lingered in the kitchen although I was no match for her. I don't know if my husband had met her before, but they must have known right away, strains of "Some Enchanted Evening," these two unhappy strangers.

Her Affair

She went to a psychiatrist because she wasn't feeling up to snuff and he recommended pills. "Oh yes, of course," she said, nodding her head obediently, but didn't go get any. Next week he asked if she was feeling at all different from the pills and she said she hadn't filled the prescription yet. He looked mad and said since she hadn't taken any pills he wouldn't treat her and would in fact never see her again, but as long as she was there they might as well talk since he was going to charge her for this session anyway. She was a little taken aback. "I had no idea they were that important to you," she said, but then had nothing to add because she had no intention of ever taking any because, well, she hated pills. Even and especially the birth-control pill, which she no longer took since her husband never slept with her anyway. That was one of the reasons she wasn't feeling so good about herself or the world either, although there were plenty of other reasons such as her failure to be a decent humorous and understanding mother to her kids as well as the fact that she had no education and a big crooked tooth and she turned everybody's everything pink in the wash and she got very very frightened while in the middle of doing nothing in particular which made her even more frightened. She could no longer even drive a car. She had taken the train to the city for this appointment.

The psychiatrist asked her what her problem was. She said her husband didn't sleep with her anymore. She said she felt like something left too long in the vegetable drawer. Then the psychiatrist told her several things, but she could only remember one. He told her to tell her husband that if he didn't get himself some help pronto she was going to go out and have an affair. "Oh," she said, laughing a very small laugh, "I could never do that."

"Time's up," he said and she paid him and she got on the train and went home and her husband was in the bathtub. The mirror was all fogged up and he was smoking grass. The bathroom smelled sweet with it. His ragged bathrobe hung on the back of the door. "How did it go," he asked, but not in a friendly voice. "Listen," she said, sliding the glass shower door open and looking down at him naked in their squarish beige tub, his penis afloat. His eyes were bloodshot and his big knees poked up from the water. "Listen. If you don't get yourself some help pronto I'm going to have an affair." Then she slid the door back and went downstairs to make a cup of tea. Later, when supper was ready, she hardly glanced at him. He took his place at the table without speaking to her, his mouth a thin line. She served a perfect brisket with carrots and turnips and potatoes.

He didn't get himself some help and she started to have an affair that very week. It turned out she couldn't wait. A businessman from up the street was very obliging, yes he would be delighted to sleep with her, and he consulted his date book directly and told her later in the week would be convenient. She called her old friend Lucky, who still lived in a small apartment on Hudson Street with two Great Danes. "Hi," she said, "could I borrow your apartment for an afternoon?" and she told him why. Lucky was happy to oblige; perhaps he had never really liked her husband. He said he would take the dogs out for three hours if she gave him a little notice. She looked forward to it very much and there was some small hassle about who could sneak away from what when and how long would the dogs be gone, because the businessman was allergic to dogs but Lucky said he'd do a little vacuuming and leave the windows open. Everybody really wanted her to have an affair. It was sort of touching.

The funny thing is now she can't remember anything about that afternoon except the Great Danes part. And they weren't even there.

She Imagines His Side

She imagines him lying in the tub, pleasantly high, enjoying the water lapping around his shoulders, the quiet house, and thinking about what—architecture? Art? Nothing at all? Suddenly she comes clomping upstairs, bursts into the bathroom, and lays this line on him. She stands there with her coat on! Then she stomps out again. What the hell is he to make of that? He frowns, shifts his weight in the tub. Did she really say what he thinks she said? He is stunned into a deeper stupor from which he is roused by the uncomfortable sensation of cooled water. There is a mealy gray scum around the tub now, old soap. His knees are cold. He turns the hot tap back on, a trickle, holds the washcloth under it, then places it upon his knees to warm them. Lights his pipe again. Inhales, closes his eyes. The house is quiet. He hears the radio faintly, which means she is in the kitchen. Rolling Stones. That's a relief. She must be cooking.

He can't take any part of her seriously. Chicken is never the same two days running. She'll make it marvelously on Monday, and three nights later it's a failure. How hard can it be to pay attention to what she is doing? Except he loves the way she holds the baby. She is so sure of that. He trusts her implicitly. It moves him to tears even. But other than that, it is hard to know what goes on in her mind, what she wants of him. What she wants. He hates it when she tries to please him, when she pretends to like something because he does. It makes him angry; worse, it irritates him. He wants an independent woman.

He wonders what she is cooking. Brisket? She's gotten quite good at brisket recently; she won't tell him what she does with it. A secret, she says, smiling, as if it mattered. Garlic? He hates tarragon and he hopes she remembers that this time. He has a bit of an appetite now. Then he remembers what she said. He stands up abruptly, water sluicing off him like a giant. He dries his feet on a scratchy little hand towel first, one toe at a time, steps onto the bath mat. He calls her name once or twice as he sees no bath towel on the towel rack. No answer. Is the music louder now? He is angry. He hates to get angry, which makes him angrier. She forces him to be angry. He shouldn't have to ask her for a towel. Things should go smoothly in a well-run household.

The towels are still in the laundry basket at the foot of the bed. So are the sheets. Last week she threw a red skirt into the wash and dyed his tennis shorts pink. She said she thought they looked nice like that. She had laughed shyly, knowing it wasn't funny. He didn't find it funny. It shows such a lack of respect for him, the way she runs the household. She has no concept of what it means to be a wife.

But don't forget, this is how she imagines it. Perhaps she has unwittingly loaded the dice in her favor.

Not Meaning to Brag

I remember one summer I was slim enough to wear a yellow polka-dot two-piece bathing suit, and still, I could see him looking sadly down the beach like a dog on a rope. No matter what, there was still only one of me.

Which later he regretted taking so long to find out.

The World Looked Different

After her husband moved out she stopped picking up. Why should she? She didn't care. They were getting divorced. It wasn't her house anyhow, as it turned out. Whole bookcases slid to the floor. Potatoes lay where they rolled to after the bag broke. She rinsed her coffee cup, wiped her spoon on her apron. Then she stopped wearing her apron. The big house took on the look of a half-eaten sandwich, waxed paper and mayonnaise everywhere. Wherever she stepped she stepped in something, or on something, or something rolled away under a table or bed. Her children were scattered. Some had no home anymore, not really. Where would they all spend Christmas? She took to wearing her nightgown all the time. Sometimes she had scary dreams. The raccoons returned to nest in the walls. Previously her husband had chased them away with hammers and nails, with traps and foul language. At her urging, it must be noted. It was she who had objected to their presence beneath (for example) the bathtub, where one of them gave birth and you could hear the unnerving scritchings of tiny claws and cooings and conversations among the family members while you lay on your back in a bubble bath trying to clear your mind. You could feel the vibrations of their little claws on the undersurface of the tub. Her husband laughed. They are only raccoons.

Raccoons have conversations. They have words and tones of voice. They laughed their little asses off. This is our house, she would say to her husband, and we are human beings. He really didn't mind the raccoons. But then he wasn't home all day worrying and he slept soundly at night when the raccoons were so active. It was she who was wakened by their carousing. Her husband had enjoyed sharing his house with wildlife. It was she who had objected to their nightly excursions and comings home at dawn drunk and disorderly, the whole huge family of them, babies too, after a night of barhopping or pool playing or whatever raccoons do in the suburbs where there isn't much to do besides root around in the neighbors' garbage. Her children also had not been too crazy about the raccoons, although she had assured them that they could not claw through the plaster and eat them in their beds. Sometimes the dog would growl at the big white walls, the hair on her back standing up. It was an unpleasant way to live. Like always being sunburned. Finally her husband had taken action grumpily and the raccoons had left the premises. It turned out to be simple. You just boarded up the hole they had made as a door before they came home in the morning. It worked. They moved into a tree in the yard.

But now she found the house lonely with everyone gone and when the raccoons returned she was almost glad to have them back, although it worried her to hear their tiny fingernails scratching on the inside of the wall behind the headboard of the bed her husband had moved down from her daughter's room; she was sleeping in the daughter's bed now; her daughter had moved in with her boyfriend; her husband had taken his own bed back to the city with him. Her children had scattered (two in boarding schools) because the house was for sale, and only she was living in it because she had nowhere else to live at the moment. After all you cannot send a woman away to boarding school. She was supposed to be looking for a job and an apartment, but sometimes she went into the city and walked around with no stockings on in the cold and then took the train back to the house, telling whoever asked that yes, she had looked all day, all day, for everything. But really she just drank coffee and smoked cigarettes and so forth while wandering around not even like a chicken with her head cut off. Not even with as much energy or purpose as that! No wonder she locked every door every night. No wonder she left little feasts for the raccoons. No wonder nobody spoke to her anymore but looked at her when she drove by, her hair uncombed, in her nightgown. Pull yourself together, they must have prayed, and after a while she did. The house got sold, and her husband had to hire a whole cleaning crew to tidy it up after she left. It was in his name; it was his house. She didn't pick anything up. She wasn't well at the time. Even now, looking back, she isn't sorry it was such a mess. The raccoons? She hopes they are still there.

No Happy Answers

She remembers her son patting his baby sister's arm. "It's okay," he whispered, trying to comfort the child. "It happened to me when I was your age too." All her children were clustered around the big white rocker where she sat. She and her second husband were explaining about the coming divorce. The house was up for sale. He had gotten himself an apartment through his university and he was moving into it soon. Where would everyone else go? There were no happy answers. She didn't know where she would be once the house was sold. Everyone needed a place to live and she needed a job. She had never lived without her kids before. But things were different now. Apartments were expensive; you couldn't live on nothing anymore. And a job? What did she know how to do besides fall in love? It was a terrible time. They decided the older kids would go away to school, and her parents agreed to pay for that. The littlest girl went to the city with her father. She was starting kindergarten. Her oldest daughter had already moved in with her boyfriend.

But It Got Better

This was when her son was away at school. A terrible
school, but cheap. Paint was peeling off the walls and
ceilings and there was a leak in the bathroom, but she left
him there anyway. At least it was someplace green. She
was getting divorced (again) and the house was being
sold and she was looking for a place to live in the city and
trying to find work. Everything was up in the air. She
knew somebody who had gone to this school. She knew
somebody who said he would keep an eye on her son for
her. She thought it would be okay. But then that person
left for Montana.

The boy was young. He was homesick. Sometimes he
called her late at night. He was in a bad way and could
hardly talk except to say couldn't he please come home.
Couldn't he live with her. He would sleep on the couch.
Or anywhere. He would be quiet. He would be good.
But she was just finding her feet. She had a job and an
apartment in the city. She told herself her son would be
better off coming home on vacations. She told herself he

needed room to run around. "Hi, honey," she would say. "How are you doing?" and she tried to sound cheerful. "Not too good," he'd answer, his voice small on the other end of the line. Then he was silent. She was silent. And there were those funny celestial sounds in the telephone wires that let you know the whole universe is out there and how big it is. "Here," she'd say then, "talk to Wes." Wes was her boyfriend. She thought maybe he could help. Man to boy. She didn't know what to say.

So the boy stayed where he was in a green place with nobody watching out for him.

Some things are so sad you think they can't get better, and nothing will be okay. She didn't make it better, although she tried, later. It got better by itself. He has a wife and a baby girl now. They sleep in the same bed. He lives on an island.

I Had a Good View

Years later I was traveling on a bus. I watched the passengers getting off somewhere fancy. A well-dressed woman and a boy greeted a man who descended from the bus carrying a briefcase. The boy stood by politely while the man greeted the woman. The man nodded to the boy and it seemed to be the moment for the boy to come forward extending his hand and so he did, but the two adults had already begun to talk and didn't notice. He stepped back again. You could sense his great eagerness. He was maybe nine or ten.

His hair was carefully combed. He was slight of build. It was Bridgehampton. He had a smile plastered to his face. He could not seem to stop expecting something warm and good to happen. He was not asking for much. I couldn't take my eyes off them and I had a good view. Then the man and woman started to walk away. The boy followed, then saw his shoe was untied, and he knelt down to attend to the lace. He soon got up, though, and half ran, half hopped, trying to catch up, looking to see if they would wait, or notice, but they did neither; he again knelt down, tied, then darted forward only to bend down and tie it again. He smiled just as if they were calling to him. He maintained his look of eagerness and expectation as if the two people, the man and the woman, were turning to see where he was, that he was still there, and that he was following close behind in the gathering dark.

Such Appetites

After we got divorced he went out with a former nun for a while. "Such appetites!" he said in wonder. "Why tell me?" I asked and hung up the phone.

Friends Again

I can't remember what made us friends again. Was there a moment in particular? I wish you were here. Was it my first grandchild? We all went to Pennsylvania. It was Christmas. I think I was already there, cooking, and you rented a car and drove with the kids. Kids, I say, although they weren't kids anymore. We all stayed together at my daughter's house in the middle of nowhere, Pennsylvania. You slept upstairs with my son; I slept downstairs on a pull-out couch with the girls. As best I can remember. We ate and ate. You had bought presents for everyone, although you had never before gone shopping for presents. We ate together at the same table again, and it wasn't your table or mine, but my daughter's. "He is a very nice baby," you said, your eyes filling with tears. There was a lot of snow; we were all together. Was that it?

And He Told Good Stories

For example once he was at a cocktail party and he was maybe thirty-five and he said to the daughter of the host, a serious child of twelve or thirteen, they were both of them standing by the door that looked out on a moonlit beach, "Will you run away with me?" and the child answered without hesitating, "Just wait while I get my shawl."

How could you not love a man who loved that story?

Married Men

Everybody (my sister is using the word loosely) goes out with one or two and then learns her lesson.

Not everybody, I say.

Not everybody what, my sister asks. Goes out with one or learns her lesson?

Both, I say. Especially learns her lesson. For that you need self-respect, which can be a long time coming.

Yep, my sister says. She is sewing. She is a quilter. She made a fifty-year anniversary quilt for our parents some years ago.

Anyway, I've been on both sides of that, I say, and both were awful.

What part of the equation stayed the same? she asks.

Um, I say, thinking she is about to accuse me of something. Like maybe I got my just deserts. What goes around comes around. Something like that.

The married man, she says.

Well, that's true, I say.

The woman is always the other woman. Whichever end you're on you're the other woman. It's a man's world, she says. Or it used to be anyway. She bites off a piece of thread. Men got used to helping themselves.

Not all of them, I say.

Not all of them, she agrees.

I was nobody's victim, I say.

We're not talking victim here. We're talking having your cake and eating it too and eating it too and eating it too.

Free to Give

But what does it all really mean, you stopped saying after our daughter was born. There was so much to do. The existential, the cosmic depression, ebbed a bit; it wasn't your daily bread anymore. Then we were divorced and you had your daughter several nights a week. A child to make breakfast for. Lamb chops to buy. You had hems to mend (with a stapler) and hair to brush and shampoo to stock up on. Often on vacations my son stayed with you. You both lay on the big soft bed together, you tousling my son's hair, talking about art. You both made art out of everything. Watermelon rind. Styrofoam. Broken clocks and chair legs. My son loved you and you loved my son. You loved my daughters. Now that nothing was expected of you, you were free to give.

Mortality

Many years later, much water under the bridge, the bridge itself having fallen into the water, my now-former second husband mentioned in passing that a certain woman had fallen ill, and he knew he should write her, but he was afraid she would write him back. And what could he say? He spoke of her as if she had been a mutual friend of ours. Although it had been years I felt an old flash of anger at her name. What could he say to her? he wanted to know. It was all so depressing, he went on, so terribly depressing. He stirred his tea. And with that gesture there were no sides anymore, no right and wrong. No *How could she? I had children! How could he!* We were only human.

We were all of us mortal.

PART TWO

Mortality

I Ate There Once

She never thought he'd get old this way. Never thought his defenses would come down one by one, dismantled, she realizes, by children. She imagines a split-rail fence coming apart over the years. He wasn't wise, she understands now, he was depressed. They both had mistaken depression for wisdom. She has married again, the third time, and she sits up front with her new husband, the nicest man in the world. Her old husband sits in back, bundled in blankets, blowing his nose in his old red kerchief, wearing his brown hat. He has gotten so gentle. Especially since she has remarried. He treats her like a flower.

They have their own language. It isn't secret, but it is their own. Certain sights carry weight for them. They remember everything. She once told him she remembered the exact moment when she knew it wouldn't last. That they weren't going to stay together, that their little vessel had not been made very well, that it had sprung too many leaks, and then in anger both of them had gouged holes in the bottom. Sink, damn you, they thought.

"I know when I knew it, but I didn't say anything. We were standing under that tree," she said. "I forget the name."

"It was a mimosa," he said. "The mimosa tree on the corner."

Today they are driving upstate to see their daughter graduate. Her new husband is driving. She loves his kind profile, the way he keeps asking her former husband if he is warm enough. It was he who remembered the extra lap rug. They are like three old friends, companionable, everybody on their best behavior. They pass a sign for a Mexican restaurant, coming up on the right. It is the only place to eat on the parkway.

"I've always wondered what kind of place that is," says her new husband, slowing down for a look as they approach. "Unlikely spot for a restaurant. The food must be terrible." The restaurant, only barely visible through trees, vanishes behind them. As it happens, it was here that she and her second husband had eaten their wedding supper, twenty-five years ago. They were by themselves and had been married about an hour.

"I ate there once," she says. Her expression doesn't change. She doesn't turn around.

"So did I," says a voice from the back.

Her Second Husband's
Lack of Beliefs

Long ago when they were first getting acquainted and he took her to St. Thomas they stood on the beach one night and he talked about rock pools and the origins of life and she thought and probably said, Oh goody, religion, you do believe in something, but he disabused her. Don't try and make anything of it, he said. A rock pool is only a rock pool for me. Not God. But she did what she could with it just the same.

Bluefish and Her Father

One day on the beach the lifeguard blew his whistle. This was maybe twenty years ago. A large dark stain was moving through the waves, easily visible, as the ocean was the color of a cut cucumber that day, or a celery leaf, the very palest green. The stain was big, irregularly shaped. It moved; it stalled. It moved again, slowly. Everybody hurried out of the water and stood on the beach staring at the green wave and the darkness in it. Then a figure burst through the crowd and barreled out into the water, right in the middle of the dark place. It was her father. Come out of there, everybody screamed, it's a school of bluefish! They're feeding! But he already knew that. He was interested in swarms and schools of things. He was interested in bees and termites and ants. He wanted to see what it felt like, he explained later, to be among them.

The Horse Chestnut

The tree is so old that the huge branches swoop down along the ground for thirty feet before rising again with their weight of green. It is mossy underfoot, spread with the tiny blue flowers my father loved. "As big as a church" was how he described this tree, and he said he was certain it was haunted. He would sit beneath it in a white chair and think his thoughts. You couldn't see him unless you stepped under the tree too. There's a photograph of my father the biologist and my second husband the physicist peering at something up in the branches of this tree. They are shading their eyes. My father seems to be saying something, pointing something out. Was a child in the branches above? Was it the way the branches themselves grew out from the enormous trunk? They were intent. They wear the good-natured expressions of people used to having an excellent time with their minds. They got along despite their differences. My father believed in the genetically programmed desire human beings have to be useful. My second husband had no such worldview; he winged it, although he had his passions. What was on their minds that afternoon? There's nobody to ask. Only the tree itself, getting ready to burst into bloom again this spring, willy-nilly.

An Elegant Theory

She and the kids were eating at the Moon Palace, the Chinese restaurant on 112th and Broadway where physicists from Columbia University used to have their feasts and scratch their theories on the backs of napkins and matchbooks. Her daughter looked up from her moo-shu vegetables and with her chopsticks indicated a man whose iron-colored hair stuck five inches out from his head like a cloud of wires. "Too much science," she said, a theory elegant in its simplicity.

Gone

Long ago she was traveling in Europe with her mother and father. Her mother had asked her to come along because her father's health was frail. Sometimes before her mother came down from the hotel room for breakfast she and her father would sit at a table and say nothing. He didn't speak to her. She tried little tidbits of conversation, but it was nothing doing. He barely looked at her, even though she was sitting right there. He picked up the paper and drank his black coffee. Maybe he was too depressed to talk. If she had it to do over, what would she say? Lighten up, Pop? Of course she doesn't have it to do over because her father is dead and gone.

He would read the newspaper and drink his coffee and not speak. Then when her mother came down he would talk. Or not. As soon as her mother appeared she herself got the holy hell out of there. He wasn't her husband after all. He was her father. She didn't have to stay there forever.

Now and then she sees him on the city street. A stranger pushes his wheelchair. For just an instant her heart turns over. It is so hard to comprehend gone.

To Keep Him Company

The night my father fell and couldn't get up and my mother couldn't get him up not being strong enough and it was four in the morning, they didn't want to disturb anyone at that hour by telephoning for help. So she lay down beside him on the floor and stayed with him until morning.

Eating Peanuts

When her father was dying and everybody was sleeping in the hospital all her third husband wanted to do was go home and he needed to and she said okay but she called him later when her father wasn't expected to live through the night. I want you to be here, she said, with me, and he came, but she was surrounded by family anyway—eleven people in the small room. Her husband was hungry as he hadn't eaten and it was one in the morning and he went out but all he could find was a can of peanuts which he ate over by the window, the can making that little pouf of escaping air as he opened the vacuum seal, and he stood munching away to keep body and soul together as quietly as he could while her father labored to die and all in all, although at first she was mad he was eating peanuts while her father died, in retrospect there was something very reassuring about the whole homely thing.

Skipping Stones

Her father had a collection of skipping stones. He kept them in a black plastic ashtray three inches in diameter, two inches high, with niches for six cigarettes. They stood on their edges from largest to smallest. They were always on his desk, wherever his desk happened to be at the moment. They must have survived a number of packings and unpackings. She doesn't know when they were first gathered, or by whom. Maybe he found them all himself. Maybe children helped, grandchildren, great-grandchildren. She imagines a small figure running to him on the beach. "Here," the child cries, handing him a smooth thin stone. "Yes," says her father, putting down his book. "That's a good one." He speaks with a Chesterfield cigarette in his mouth. He tests the weight, the feel of the stone in his hand. He makes the sideways motion of skimming. "Perfect," he says finally. "You going to keep it?" the child asks solemnly. Her father nods. This image seems quite clear to her. She likes to think this is a real memory, but she doesn't know that she isn't making it up.

Still, here are the stones. Someone chose each one. Maybe he collected them all himself. She likes that idea too. She likes to imagine him obsessed all one summer, head bent as he walked at the water's edge, stooping to pick up one stone after another until he had enough, or his pockets could hold no more, or his mind moved on to something else. She thinks she can remember such a time, not so terribly long ago. But she can't be sure. The only thing she is sure of is the beach, it is always the same beach at the end of the same road where they went as a family summer after summer. Much has changed, but the water still glitters in the distance at the end of that road, and his grandchildren are on that beach where she once played, and his great-grandchildren.

When he died, her father's secretary wrapped each stone separately in a paper towel and sealed it with Scotch tape and sent them to her in a big manila envelope with the ashtray at the bottom. She didn't open them. Sometimes she took one out and felt its shape through the paper and put it back again. She couldn't open them. She wanted the moment to be right; she didn't want to do this just any-time; she was waiting to feel in the exact center of some-thing. Meanwhile, as long as she didn't unwrap them, there was something of her father still to come.

In the end of course there was just the unexceptional afternoon she sat on the couch and unwrapped every sin-gle stone, unceremoniously dumping the paper on the floor while the small pile of stones grew on her lap. They were so ordinary, so beautiful—gray, blue-gray, mauve, black, taupe. The color of stone. The largest is three inches at its widest, the smallest a boomerang shape not much bigger than a peanut shell. She remembered skip-ping stones as a kid, how you can hear the tiny thud each jump makes, and you realize for the first time how taut is the surface of water, and it is magic that you have sent a stone to do this amazing thing, to skip six, seven times, almost like flying. She set them up in the ashtray as her father had.

As far as she knows her father collected nothing else. He had music, of course, and books, he had poems by heart and words he loved. He had favorite stories and people and moments, but he didn't collect things for their thingness. The stones were the only things her father saved for themselves. They comfort her. Something she can hold in her hand.

Sufficient Information

One day she thought to herself, I can do this, I can live without a man. She had been doing this for almost twelve years. She was good at it. She preferred it to doomed love. She was tired of relationships whose greatest intimacy consisted of sitting up all night weeping while love died. But she thought, Well, I will give it this one last try, and she placed an ad in a certain bookish journal. If nothing comes of it, she thought, then I will live happily by myself. After all she had her kids and her grandchildren and her friends. Her life was full. When she began to get the answers there was one in particular that had very nice handwriting. It was firm and direct and it slanted upward, a sign of optimism. The letter read, in part, that he thought life went better by twos. In her ad she had specified a nice man, and he wrote that he thought he was nice, but that this wasn't something you could say about yourself, not really. She took a deep breath and she called him up. He was broiling a piece of salmon when she called but dropped everything to talk. They met in the rain a few days later; they had a Chinese meal. They met again for supper. And again. Thirteen days later he asked her to marry him. Yes, she said, standing in the kitchen doorway. It was as simple as that.

Her Third Husband

The second time they saw each other he came to her house with two pounds of chopped meat, an onion, a slice of bread, a small can of V8, and a bottle of chili sauce. He asked if she had an egg and she said that she thought so somewhere. In his breast pocket he had a recipe for meat loaf and he laid it on her counter as he unpacked the ingredients. She examined it. It was his mother's recipe, written in pen on a piece of loose-leaf paper: Billie's Meat Loaf. She felt her heart stirring. He grated the onion. She had always chopped hers but said she thought grating was a terrific idea. Tears flowed from both their eyes and she turned on the oven fan and when that wasn't enough she opened a window. He set the slice of bread in a bowl and poured the V8 on top. She watched everything he did, her hands behind her back. Her job was mashed potatoes and she could do this with both eyes closed. She had peeled them already and set them in the pan of cold water, a little salt in the water, the fire on low. Butter and cream were ready and her old masher with the wooden handle. They both liked frozen peas and that took about five seconds to prepare. Now this is the best part, he said as he rolled up his sleeves and dug his hands in the bowl full of meat and bread and tomato juice and onion. She had already lit the oven—once his had exploded because he let the gas go too long while he hunted for a match. (He had told her that story the first time they met, four nights ago. He had come all the way up to her neighborhood. It was raining and he carried such a nice big umbrella. She herself couldn't lay hands on an umbrella from one day to the next.) When he had shaped the meat loaf in the roasting pan he poured the whole bottle of chili sauce over the top. I use ketchup, she said, but the chili sauce is a very good idea. Nice for tang. Are you sure thirty minutes is enough? she asked. That's an awful lot of meat loaf. But he didn't want to leave it too long in the oven as he liked it very rare. They exchanged raw-meat stories. I've eaten raw meat all my life, she said, the first time I met my first son-in-law I was putting a dripping gobbet of raw flank steak into my mouth. He was afraid to shake my hand and I don't blame him. She laughed heartily at the memory, reminding herself of the insect world and how it treats the husbands. He laughed too, but not uneasily because he also loved raw meat. (This was before salmonella.) You know, he said, when I first heard your laugh on the phone I thought you might weigh three hundred pounds. I hope you don't mind my saying that. Then of course they kissed for a long time as she leaned back against the counter. It was very very nice. They were both middle-aged and free. His shirt was clean and blue, his jacket frayed and respectable. She was wearing several layers of things and found herself suddenly as pleased with her own shape as he was. At some point in the evening feeling especially joyous he said he had all kinds of funny thoughts in his mind. Like what, she asked. Oh, he said, it's too embarrassing. Like what, she said. Oh well, sometimes when I'm walking down the street I wonder if there were a terrible drought would I be able to drop to my knees and lap dog urine. You know, to save my life? Isn't that funny, she said, so do I! So do I!

They were a perfect couple.

Insomnia

She has had insomnia and her husband has also had insomnia and she has decided it is the mattress so they go to the store and she lies down on one mattress after another and he will not. This is because he is too dignified to get in a prostrate position in a public place with his shoes resting on the plastic they use to cover the lower part of the mattress. Each mattress she lies down on she likes better than the last. "Lie down," she says to him, "you're going to be on it for the rest of your life after all." But he doesn't want to. Perhaps because of the salesman looking on. But finally he does, then gets right up again. "It's fine," he says, "get whichever one you like." So they buy it and it comes that very night. But now it is four in the morning and she is still awake while her husband breathes regularly and sweetly beside her. When she tires of listening to him breathe, which takes a long time because he sounds like a child and it is beautiful to hear, she comes into the other room and looks out her window uptown and at the lights on the river. Now and then opening a can of tuna fish and thinking this fish in this room on 112th Street was originally swimming in the deep Atlantic and now it is here on the thirteenth floor. What a miracle, although not for the fish. Still. You can appreciate things at four in the morning that would go right past you during the day.

Social Security

She had to go to the Social Security office because there was confusion over her name. She had returned to her maiden name, and it all needed sorting out. They needed proof that she was herself again. It was a matter of documentation. She needed her birth certificate, her divorce papers. Her husband, who was trying to help, upon perusing this first set of papers, said, "I didn't know you'd had a Mexican divorce," which sent her back to the night twenty-seven years ago when she had lain weeping while the radio played. She was with the man she was going to marry, the man who was going to be her second husband, they were in a rented house in the gloomy Northwest Woods of Long Island. *Abbey Road* had just come out. If he had asked her why she was crying she wouldn't have known what to say. But he hadn't, thank God, he had just let her cry. This was a kindness on his part; he had just let her be. It was the eve of her flight to Mexico; she was twenty-seven years old. It was not that she'd wanted to stay with her first husband. Life had seemed to have sadness mixed into everything she touched.

But now, clutching all these documents, she got herself on the subway and went downtown. It took a while to find the office and a while longer to get in the elevator. She had claustrophobia and could not ride alone. Then a messenger appeared and when she explained her problem he said he would take her to six even though he was only going to two. He said he knew somebody else who felt the same way about elevators, and she said "Thank you" and tried not to stare at his thighs in their nylon tights. "Goodbye," she said at six, "and thank you again."

Once inside the office she found the right line to stand on and sooner than she expected she was explaining her presence to a man behind what may or may not have been a bulletproof screen. He looked at her papers and said he could fix it one-two-three, but it would take a few days. He made copies of everything. "Is that it?" she asked. She didn't have much faith in the system, although it hadn't failed her personally. "That's it," he said and waved the next person over. So it was time to leave again, and again because of claustrophobia she pretended to be absorbed in studying the wall while one after another the elevators came and went with nobody in them. Then an old man shuffled over, someone she hadn't noticed before, and he was saying goodbye to everybody and they all said goodbye to him. It appeared that he worked there, or had once worked there and still came in; that was what she made of it.

They chatted in the elevator about the weather. Downstairs in the lobby he unexpectedly linked his arm through hers and told her he would walk her to the corner. This seemed gallant of him. He was an old man and very clean shaven, his eyes were clear, although watering a bit in the cold, and he wore a pale scarf and a porkpie hat. He told her he had written the music to many shows but had had no luck yet having them produced. He mentioned disappointments at the hands of wealthy men whose family names she recognized. She nodded and clucked. She was a grandmother but perhaps looked younger in her new green hat. He enjoyed talking to her. Then she looked down and noticed that his shoes were old and cracked and the trousers he was wearing, visible under his coat, were stained with what looked like whitewash running in streaks down to the cuffs. She felt disoriented. There she was with her three names but one person surely, and there he was with a poor person's clothes on, yet he spoke so clearly and smelled fine. He left her on the street and she watched him heading into a warm building that contained the coffee shop where he worked on his music, and she made her way to the subway wishing she had asked him to tell her the names of some of his songs. Her mother had that very morning called to ask if she knew the words to "Hindustan," which she did not. Then her mother called back. "I have an idea," she said. "We will write new words to this tune. Nobody will know, because they are all dead, and we will make our fortune. Just change 'Hindustan' to something else."

She thinks about it now, maybe it wasn't such a bad idea, since she will never see any Social Security what with the confusion over her names, and now she thinks she may have missed her chance, having allowed the old man to disappear. Perhaps next time she has to go down (because she has no faith in the system) she will run into him again. Her mother often calls her in the early morning asking, "Do you know the words to," and then she'll sing a line of a song like "Just give me something to remember you by," and then the lyric and the tune stay in her mind all day, thus ruining it with sadness and pity. As she puts the divorce papers away she wonders if perhaps the old man had written "Laura" or "Tangerine" or something else she might once have known.

Ponds

She used to feel bad for the swans that lived on little ponds and marshes off the turnpike surrounded by tin cans and old tires, although corporations pledged they were keeping the water clean and the swans seemed to be enjoying themselves. Still she thought it was awful to have to be a swan in Elizabeth, New Jersey. Then as she got older she realized it was okay. Clean water was clean water no matter what surrounded it, right? And a pond in the middle of garbage was still a pond. For some reason this was on her mind today, the word "pond" especially, such a beautiful word, and she was floating on the surface of the idea of it all morning hoping it would get her out of her poor mood, her piss-poor mood not to put too fine a point on it. A mood that came from nowhere, and settled on her like soot. Instead of a pond she saw a man relieving himself on the sidewalk, and the odd contrast between the shabbiness of his garments and the incredible force of the urine startled her and she allowed herself to be cheered up by how well his innards were working. A sign of life. When she related this to her daughter, her daughter said, "I hate it when men pee on the street because you always have to see their rubbery little penises and I really don't want to see one unless I really want to see one." They both found this very funny and laughed out loud in their separate cities.

This afternoon from the Broadway bus her eye is caught by the little tiny diamond bulbs making up stars on the ceiling of the Fred Astaire Dance Studio, and she can even see two people dancing, the woman light in the man's arms, they dance in and out of sight. In the window, she sees two young men in black trousers and white shirts who stand at the ready should there be a partnerless woman to squire. "Shhh," she wants to say to her husband as he speaks a pleasantry in her ear, "I am remembering being lonely." He continues to speak as the bus lowers itself with a wheezing sound for an elderly passenger, like an elephant kneeling. If I were lonely and not happily married and feeling okay about myself but in need of warmth I could do worse than go there and pay for dance lessons, she thinks, still looking at the starry ceiling. Body warmth is body warmth, a young and handsome lad is still a pleasure even if you are not going to partake of him in the time-honored way. For a moment she imagines being held in a store-bought young man's arms and somehow it's all tied up with the pond and swans and the old things, she herself being the old thing although not discarded surely like rusty cans or flat tires (here she squeezes her husband's hand), and you have to take gladly what life offers, she has learned that much, and sometimes you get lucky. There's nothing wrong with that, is there? There's nothing wrong with that.

This Thanksgiving

My husband says he's tired but won't lie down on the green couch where our friend, my former husband, lay last year. He doesn't want to stir up sad memories, he says. What if the kids look at him and think of our friend? The room is full of absence. I crack an egg and beat it with a little water. I add this to the cornbread, breaking it with my hands. The oven is preheating. I add rosemary, which I forgot, to the onions, and stir. Then I walk over and give him a kiss.

What Goes through the Mind
While Stripping the Meat
from the Bones

She puts all the dark meat in her mouth. The dark meat is her favorite and also the wings. She is something of a pig. Her hair tickles her face, but her hands are too full of turkey fat to scratch her forehead. The word "carcass" sounds see-through, raggedy, frail. Its ribs exposed. If you scrape out the stuffing too zealously you get bitter bits, innards to spit into your napkin. Long ago she'd have stuck the whole thing in the icebox and hoped for the best. Then thrown it out. The thought of turkey soup too awful to contemplate. But now that we are all grown-up and happy, she thinks, we save the meat for sandwiches, throw out the bones. Our thoughts are grateful if not cheerful, for we have much to be thankful for. We are still alive and still talking to one another. Voices from four generations fill the room.

Except of course your chair was empty. So was the couch you lay on last year with blankets heaped over you and children of all ages asking if they could get you anything. You were shivering. You were glad you had come.

"Go," said your doctor. "Yes, you can make the trip. Go. It will be good for you." It was to be your last Thanksgiving, something nobody imagined, certainly not me, I thought we had a year or more and in a year anything can happen. Cures can be found. Strength regained. But you died instead.

Where Are the Kids

Where are the kids? my sister wants to know.
  I can't write about the kids, I say uneasily.
  But they are part of this, she says. Their lives.
  Their lives are their own, I say.
  They are wonderful, my sister says, I love your kids.
  I know, I say. They are the nicest people I know.
  But I don't see them in here very much, my sister says.
  This is not about that, I say.
  Not about what, she asks.
  Not about holding them up to the light, I say.
  They should be here.
  But they are everywhere, I say, they are on every page.
Don't you see?
  See what?
  They are the whole point.

Weather

This is my favorite weather, rain and wind whistling between the buildings. I don't feel I should be somewhere else. I don't feel guilty for staying where I like best to be. I'm happy to be home, dropping the chicken into cold water with celery and carrots, preparing my dumplings. I should be finding bowls and spoons and setting the table. This is the weather for golden soup.

This is what you won't be here for. Your daughter's life. The new Japanese movie at the Film Forum. All the April birthday parties. Grandchildren growing up. Tonight's rain. Tomorrow morning. A cup of tea.

Impatience

She is such a harridan. She can feel a fishwife inside her, screaming to get out, getting out! Climbing out of her shirtfront, a huge screaming fishwife. Part fish even. (She must have been one once.) She likes the sound of it, fishwife, as if she were married to a trout. Get under the rock, she was unable to scream when she was a fish. Get into the reeds! What a relief to be able to shout now, to tell them what to do; before she only had gills and a mouth that opened and shut in wonder or to take in food. They never listened to her before. She imagines fish tails diving back into her bosom, wet fish bodies reminiscent up and down her human flesh.

Today she was impatient with her husband. Sometimes she doesn't know what gets into her. It's the fishwife. She snapped at him for no reason and she is sorry and he is quiet. He is much nicer than she is in many ways, although ironically she is more tolerant. And the poor man is throwing out his mother's stuff, some of it anyway, although a lot more is going up to the attic to be covered with sheets, because her son says that keeps everything cool. They looked at all the spoons today, really beautiful spoons, and she wants to use them. Ditto the pretty candlesticks. We can put them on the table, she said to him this morning. His mother died a month ago or more, at the age of ninety-eight. She will try to be nicer and not get that awful way. After all, she is not the only one who has lost someone.

Tonight her husband has seen something about the effects of tea. You are drinking too much tea, he says. It makes you cranky. She bridles. I am just tired, she says. No really, he goes on. You had seven cups this afternoon. Tea can give you osteoporosis, and caffeine has all sorts of ill effects, and tea has a lot of caffeine. I read it, do you want to see the article? He rummages around. I don't want to see the article, she says. I don't believe anything I read anywhere. Don't be silly, he says kindly. Would you rather I drank Manhattans? she asks. She is lying in bed, four pillows behind her. Her hair has been taken down from all its barrettes and it looks (she imagines) as if she were lying in a haystack. That is not the alternative, he says. Yes it is, she snaps. Yes it is. His back is to her now. He has gone to hang something up in his closet. Quiet again. A man married to a fishwife.

Tea! She can't even have tea now? Fuck this shit, she says, and turns over to try to sleep.

Tomorrow

Tomorrow it's a year since you died. I don't seem to be able to do a damn thing today. Not a damn thing yesterday either. I start something and drop it. I walk from room to room. I eat whatever is lying out on the counter and today it's apple cake. I eat piece after piece. You weren't here for this cake; I found the recipe after you died. You wouldn't have liked it, though, you preferred my sponge cakes, light and drier. "I think your other cakes are better," you'd have said with authority. I'd have wanted to scream.

Where are you? One year.

Witness to His Life

"I want a witness to my life," he used to say. "That's all."

"That's not all," I'd say, "you also want a cook and a tailor, you want a housekeeper and a dry-cleaning establishment. You want a gourmet cook and a Kama Sutra expert and a dog walker. You want somebody to tidy up after you and love doing it. You want somebody to dance for you while the chicken is cooking."

"Not anymore." He paused and smiled. "Is that so much to ask? You liked to dance and as I recall you were rather good at it."

"You know what I mean."

"No," he'd insist. "I'm a very simple man, really. I'm easygoing. I just want a witness to my life."

One time after we'd been divorced about five years he invited me out to breakfast. We went to Tom's Restaurant or the College Inn or somewhere else lousy. He looked at me mournfully across the table. "Do you think you're ready now to run a household?" he asked.

"Is that a proposal?" I asked. "Because it's not very romantic."

"Do you?" He wore a look of dread on his face.

Maybe he was afraid I'd say yes.

When He Told Her

She didn't really believe it, not really, not in her heart of hearts. "It turns out I have something rather serious the matter with me," he said, but they were at Ollie's, on her plate a scallion pancake, on his some crispy duck. All around them the students were chattering and eating. There was the happy clatter of dishes, the smell of Chinese food. Outside all the noise of upper Broadway, buses and so forth. She knew he was telling her something monumental, something huge, but it just wasn't sinking in. Besides, the new hot tea had arrived, and the shrimp with snow peas, and she was busy opening five sugars, as she liked her tea very sweet. It was hard to hear really, to catch the drift.

He didn't use the word "cancer." He used the words "platelets" and "bone marrow." He used the words "eighty percent" and "research." He used the words "specialist" and "experimental drugs" and "trust." He didn't seem afraid, and he didn't want to alarm her. He seemed intent only on having her understand what was happening to him, what might or might not be around the corner. After all, they had been married once. But it was in this very restaurant that she had years ago asked him to explain about the solar system. To explain about the solar system and the galaxies and which was bigger, and which was older and what was still forming, and as he'd spoken she had drawn in her notebook a bunch of suns and stars and planets and moons with arrows in order to keep straight what was what and what revolved and what got revolved around. Gravity and the moon's pull, and all the rest of it. She had wanted to know where she stood exactly, and what was going on out there. He had explained it all carefully and clearly. So now as he talked about his disease, she realized that she'd forgotten everything she'd wanted so badly to remember, and the stars were swirling in all directions inside her head, and nothing was where it belonged. And after a while she reached across the table and she touched his sleeve and he grabbed her hand and held it fiercely.

"What can happen," she asked.

"Well, probably nothing for a good long while," he said, "the disease isn't active right now." He didn't say "in remission." "Nothing is going on right now, and they can't treat it until it becomes aggressive."

"What's the worst that can happen?" she asked. His eyes were hazel. She loved this man she had been so unhappy with.

"Well, we've all got to go sometime." He shrugged and laughed.

"No, I mean it."

"You can't clot," he said, "among other things, your

blood can't clot. The slightest bruise, even just your organs moving against each other in the normal course of a day, can make you bleed to death."

"That won't happen to you," she said, and held his hand really tightly.

His Cosmic Joke

Sometimes when they were out walking together, he would nod meaningfully at some very old man and whisper to her, *"Un vieux,"* as if it were the punch line of a long cosmic joke.

What It Was Called

For the longest time she couldn't remember the name of
his disease, and things went on as usual. She and her husband often had him for supper, and when he seemed tired
they walked him home, one on either side. He got exhausted going up the hill on 116th. She and her husband
told him they were tired too, that it was a steep hill. "And
it's winter," she'd hear herself say, "and we're wearing all
these heavy clothes!" Then one morning he asked if she
would mind going with him to the doctor. He was very
short of breath these days, nobody knew why, and today
they were doing a bone marrow biopsy and he was afraid
he might be tired, too tired to hail his own taxi. It might be
a long wait, but would she mind terribly going with him?
Of course not. They went together, like husband and
wife, which of course they had once been. "Why didn't
you ask me before?" she demanded.

"I didn't want to trouble you," he answered. She was
angry and sad. She wished he had asked her sooner. Then
they got out of the elevator and she saw what the sign on

the wall said: ONCOLOGY. Even then she couldn't believe it. She thought there must be a mistake, that his disease was probably some distant relation, some third cousin once removed, and it was just coincidence that they were on this particular floor. But as the hours went by and she saw the other patients, and the faces of the people who sat with them, she understood.

Myelodysplasia, she made him tell her again, and this time she remembered it.

Coming Home Tomorrow

Almost spring, and he was in the hospital. He had been there months but was coming home at long last. This or that was still very wrong, he didn't know, but the doctor had promised tomorrow for certain. She looked at him in the bed, his flesh, the way his arms had gotten all soupy, she saw that he couldn't really get up at all anymore or hardly even raise his arm right, but she had rented the wheelchair and there was oxygen at home. She found herself feeling very business-like all of a sudden. She ticked things off a list. He didn't look so wonderful, but he had been through a lot. She didn't want to get sucked into a bad sad place, all sentimental; she needed her wits about her; she wasn't even married to him anymore for god's sake. She did however love him. She looked at him again. So many transfusions, who wouldn't look exhausted? He was coming home tomorrow, glad to be home finally after months that had started out as overnight. Spring was coming sooner or later. "We will take you in the wheelchair," she said, "until you get your strength back, we will go to Ollie's," she said, "or the Thai place. I am good at wheelchairs," she said, "and we will sit in the park."

He turned his mouth down and frowned. This particular face always made her laugh. "It's just until you get your strength back," she said, although she had her doubts. The next year or two would be in a wheelchair, she was pretty damn sure. He was losing ground. But he would accommodate himself, he had been so patient through all this terrible stuff. He never complained, never. He had a year left, certainly, maybe two? She didn't know. The doctors were vague when you could find them. She was brisk; she was more than ready to go. She was collecting the heavy books to take now, so the load would be lighter tomorrow. "What's that funny look you're giving me?" she asked. He tried to smile. He had had a bad dream. It was still real and he had to ask her something. He wasn't sure it was a dream at all. And now, looking at her, he trailed off.

"What dream?" she asked.

"I dreamed," he said, his voice a little husky, "that you were leaving. I dreamed you were going away." His eyes were suddenly sharp. That old look of his. "Are you?"

"Am I what?"

"Leaving."

"What are you talking about?" She was standing at the foot of his bed now. "Don't be silly."

"It was a terrible dream," he said, "the worst dream I've ever had."

"But I'm not going anywhere. How could you think such a crazy thing?" She put the books on the chair.

"In my dream," he went on, "I was the most articulate

I've ever been in my life. I had ten reasons why you couldn't go, and I told them to you. I have never been so fluent, so eloquent, so persuasive."

She was smiling, moved in spite of her desire not to be moved. And curious. "What were they?" she asked, resting her hand on his left foot.

"I can only remember the first one."

"What was it?"

He looked at her fiercely. "We need you."

"Well, I need you too," she said, anxious to feel as little as possible, "and I wouldn't go anywhere. How could you think I would leave?" She felt like doing a little nervous jig just to show how silly he was.

"Well, you look so beautiful. I thought you must have a lover. I thought you were running away with a lover." He looked so tired.

"Oh god," she said, shaking her head. "When do you think I'd have time for a lover? I don't want a lover. I love my husband. I love my family. I love you. I'm not going anywhere. I would never go anywhere. Don't worry. You don't have to worry about that ever."

"Do you promise?" He had never asked her, Do you promise.

"I promise," she said, putting her hand on his ankle. It felt so swollen.

She didn't then crawl into bed next to him under the tangle of wires and lines hooked up to bags of blood and water, she didn't crawl into bed next to him and feel the length of her body along the length of his, although she thought about it, how she could, if she were careful, put her arm around him and her face against his cheek, how she might say, Don't you know if I were to run away it would only be with you, which she knew would please him, whether he believed it or not; she saw herself doing these things but she didn't do them. Instead she straightened up and said out loud, "Well, that's enough of that," and she walked around the bed and kissed his forehead. "I will see you tomorrow."

"You're leaving?"

"I'll see you tomorrow," she said. "Bright and early." She could tell he was still in his awful dream, but what could she say to him that she hadn't already said at one time or another? After all, she had her life to live, her errands to run, the hospital was such a difficult trip for her, and it was really the whole day, not just the hours she spent there, but the hours preparing and the rest of the day trying to forget. He had trouble lifting his arms and could no longer really sit up, but it didn't occur to her what this meant, what this signaled, that the body was dying, he had been bleeding everywhere, so many transfusions. It was over. Perhaps it is a blessing that she didn't know. The mind pulls a blindfold out of its pocket on these occasions maybe.

"So you aren't leaving us?" he asked once more, an unfamiliar look on his face. This was not a man to do any pleading. "It really was just a dream?" This was so unlike him.

The next day the nurse said, "He has children, hasn't he? Isn't there a daughter?"

And even then she didn't understand. "Do you mean I should call her?" she asked, shocked.

"He isn't stable," said the nurse.

"Should I call?" she repeated. "You mean it's time to call everyone?"

"He isn't stable," said the nurse again, kindly but firmly, and it sank in.

. . .

She thinks of his dying as a hole he fell through, a hole in the day that opened and then closed back over him. But he is still here; she feels him near. She feels him all the time. She assumes he knows now, everything she meant to say. She hopes so anyway.

Once they walked down Broadway and passed the church on 114th whose message board often quoted Woody Allen (90 PERCENT OF LIFE IS JUST SHOWING UP), but on that particular day it was blank. "Look," he'd said, surprise in his voice, "the Presbyterians have run out of things to say." He put his arm around her shoulders (he was still able to walk then). "You appreciate me," he'd said then. But maybe you had to be there. She had been there; he had been there; they had been there together.

The Animal They Made

Once they were no longer married he was free to love her again and she was free to love him too so after a while they did. Because they had always loved each other, and because of the animal they made. Not a real animal, nothing born in a litter, nothing fashioned out of clay or wood or brass, and not the beast with two backs, but what they were, the two of them together. The animal they made, that's the only way she can describe it. An animal with its own life, its own life history, its own life span. Its own intelligence. Its own memories and regrets. Its own sins. An animal with its eyes and ears open, so alive, so alive. Greeting them! Making jokes out of thin air.

Extinct now.

Drifting Away

You died, and the past separated itself from me like a continent drifting away.

PART THREE

Here and Now

The New Year

Like a trick floor. Somebody has tilted it and I have slid into the new year but you remained behind. Last night I dreamed you'd moved to California and I'd forgotten to get your number. Forgotten to call you. I was just starting to make a few inquiries when suddenly you returned, thinner and happy. I was glad to see you looking so well, although I worried about the weight you'd lost. "I've been trying to call you," I began to say. "I've been home all along," you said, "although last night might have presented problems." By which I knew you had fallen in love with somebody. You were so calm. And then this morning your ashes are still here, in a box on my bookcase.

Rocking Chair

I saw a chair you'd love, says her third husband, want to come see? It's in the street. She goes. She does love it. She starts to drag it home. What are you doing? he asks, aghast. But he has known her these ten years. I'm taking it home, of course, she says. What did you think? She doesn't understand the question. I love this, she goes on, look at the old red velvet, look at the curve of the arm, look at the broken rocker on the left, look at the original sawdust and horsehair. This is a beautiful beautiful chair, my grandma had one just like it. But where will you put it, he asks, and look, he says pointing, what is that? Horsehair! she cries delighted. That's the horsehair! That's how you know it's old. She thinks of grandmas, she thinks of rocking. Horsehair! He shudders.

It won't fit through the door, he says, but it does. It won't fit through the hall, he says, but it does. It won't fit in the study, he says, but she is determined. She makes it fit, nudging aside the other chairs, all in various states of disrepair.

It is so beautiful, she says finally, look at those lovely arms, look at the grace of the thing.

Look at the broken frame, he says, look at the stuffing and the sawdust trail through the living room. Look at this room!

But I love it, she says. I'll get it fixed.

It will cost five hundred dollars, he says.

But we got it for free, she reminds him. What did you think? she asks. You knew I would love it. What did you think? That I could just leave it there on the street?

In bed he says, Snakes. Spiders.

What? she says. It is very dark in their room.

Snakes, he says. We'll wake up and there will be snakes in there.

What? She is laughing now. Snakes don't come in chairs.

Spiders then, he says.

Don't be ridiculous, she says. It's a beautiful chair, why did you show it to me?

I wish I hadn't, he says.

What did you think? That I could leave it there? On the street? To be rained on?

It's been rained on, he says. Snakes, he says again, like a little boy. Half an hour passes. She listens to him breathing. He is not asleep. Okay, she says, poking him. I don't have to have it. They put on their bathrobes and slippers. They drag it out together. Goodbye chair, she says.

That's how much she loves him. He is happy. He vacuums up the little trail of sawdust from their pretty red rug.

Grateful

She used to think she needed to know things to be the mother. How to fix things, make everything better. And she couldn't, she just didn't know how. She felt sometimes not like a mother but like an older sister with an impatient streak. But one weekend when her oldest daughter was afraid she was losing her baby, she spoke to her son-in-law on the telephone. Shyly she asked him, "Do you think I should come?"

"My wife needs her mother," said her son-in-law, and in that second she understood all at once and forever everything she needed to know. And she got on the bus directly and went out to their house and she sat by her daughter's bed and held her hand. She stayed in the room until her daughter fell asleep and she was there when her daughter woke. She is grateful forever to him for saying the right thing at the right moment because her life changed right there on that dime. And the baby is fourteen years old. Hallelujah.

The Mothers of New York

Is it her or are the mothers of New York paying less attention? It seems every day she has to place her body between a child and the busy street, the young mothers distracted by conversation or worse. She herself can't bear anyone under thirty to get within three feet of the curb. Some head off drunkenly in its direction. On their tiny tricycles! Wearing little red bonnets! Jingling their small shiny bells! She doesn't touch these children; she plants herself in their path, a formidable object, a movable unclimbable hill, a grandmother statue. Are times simply more lax? Was she this negligent? Are young mothers more trusting than they should be? Or is she getting old?

Her memory (poor) is that she watched her children carefully on the street. It was much later that her gaze wandered. At least she kept them safe in infancy! Of course things were different then. Dangers weren't omnipresent. But about traffic she remembers being consistently alert. Don't you know, she wants to tell the mothers, don't you see? So much is so unpredictable, she wants to draw them aside and explain. Later there will be nothing you can do, having done it already or not.

Although she does love determination in the young. She smiles remembering the little girl she saw earlier who forced her mother to carry her by one arm down the block, her feet off the sidewalk, kicking and screaming the whole way, her feet in white socks and little patent-leather shoes. Now that is the perfect attire of a really good tantrum, she thinks, a little black velvet dress with lace collar and little white socks with frilly tops. Mary Janes complete the outfit. She can see the catalog now. Dress your child for a tantrum. The little boy gazing up at her as she guards the curb looks at her curiously. He is a perfect gentleman on his set of big wheels.

Wattles

Should we get our wattles done? I ask my sister. We are looking at recent snapshots.

I've heard of this thing where they freeze it, she says. No snippy-snip.

Freeze what? I say. There are several photos of me from the side. Close-up. I slide them into my palm and then into my pocket.

Freeze your wattle. First they grab one side of your chin and inject it, then they grab the other side and inject it, and presto your wattle's gone.

I have spilled my coffee. Gone? Where does it go?

It just shrinks right up. Now I know you're not going to like the sound of this, but they paralyze the muscle so it doesn't sag. She pauses. The bicycle man she likes has just entered the café. We watch him for a while. The line is long and slow in here. Plenty of time to stare. Only one person is manning the cappuccino maker this morning. The bicycle man is unaware of us, two middle-aged ladies at a table on the side.

You know, I say, regarding the guy thoughtfully, his problem is he doesn't have an ego problem.

Yeah, says my sister, but look at his nice little ass.

We observe some more. He's probably French, I say, there are Gitanes in his T-shirt pocket. You're just getting nostalgic for Paris.

He reminds me of Jean Gabin, she says.

I don't recall Jean Gabin in Lycra, I say. The man gets his coffee and we fall silent as he passes on his way out the door. We return to the subject at hand.

Anyway, it's not my muscle that's sagging, I say. I don't have muscle under my chin.

Well, whatever it is. I saw it advertised somewhere. It's called bo-tux or something.

What is "bo" short for. "Botulism"? Ha-ha, I say.

I don't think they would inject you with botulism, she says. Anyway, whatever it is it's dead.

God, I don't want anything dead injected into me.

That's what immunizations are, dummy, all that stuff's dead! And then your body forms antibodies. God! She looks at me critically. I am familiar with this look. You're so ignorant!

I know. I need that Eyewitness Book about the body.

Too advanced for you, she says, my little sister.

Power

She was sixteen and wearing a tight yellow sweater. It had shrunk, but she had to go to school and nothing else was clean. Her route was along Washington Mews, up University to Fourteenth Street, along Fourteenth to Third Avenue, then up Third to Fifteenth, then one more block east to school. It was a warm fall day. I believe she was also wearing a short plaid skirt, A-line, and probably loafers and no socks. She never could find socks. The men in New York City, where she had just moved, stared. Some of them put down their tools or else just held them slackly as she walked by. They murmured. My god, she realized. I have power. Like most power it was both utterly real and utterly illusory. But she spent the next forty years with her eye on who was looking back. This didn't get in her way. It was her way. Her ambition was to be desired. Now it's over and what a relief. Finally she can get some work done.

Nothing Is Wasted

She is a writer and she teaches writing. Well, not *teaches* writing because you can't do that, but you can certainly locate the interesting, you can go over the page with sandpapered fingertips and say, Here, what is really going on here, and if you're lucky the writer blushes and says, Oh I thought I could just skip over that part, which means you have discovered a gold mine, and you say, No, sorry, you're going to have to write it. You can point out the promising. You can encourage and allow and permit and make possible. She gives assignments so nobody has to face the blank page alone with the whole blue sky to choose from. After all she knows how hard it is to make it up from whole cloth; everybody needs a shred of something to start with to cover their nakedness and so to this end she wanders around the city with her eyes and ears open. On the subway one afternoon she sees a man holding what appears to be a silver Buddha. Good lord, she wonders, what is he doing with that? Is he going to sell it? Is she going to buy it? Where did a silver Buddha come from? Then as she is watching he brings it toward his mouth and bites off the head. How completely baffling until she sees it is not a Buddha but something edible, some sort of wafer wrapped in silver paper. Perhaps chocolate. Nevertheless, she tells her class that night, Write two pages in which somebody is eating something unusual on the bus. Write two pages, she says, in which somebody can't stop apologizing. Two pages in which somebody kills something with a shoe. Two pages containing a French horn, an ear infection, and a limp. Describe somebody by what they can't take their eyes off. Two pages. Two pages in which someone is inappropriately dressed for the occasion. And so forth. Nothing goes to waste.

What I Can't Resist

At this moment my grandson is asleep on the floor of my room; I can see his beautiful high forehead, his cowlick, and part of his left hand. The rest of him is under a patchwork quilt. He lies on the old egg-crate mattress doubled over. He likes it better than the stiff red couch. He comes visiting with his own soft pillow. This time there are no stuffed animals and he has forgotten his red nightshirt and toothbrush. Instead he has packed tiny little pewter armies, assembled and painted painstakingly with the finest of brushes. He has shown me the brush; it can't be more than three or four hairs thick. With this he has painted eyebrows, eyes beneath the visors. I need a magnifying glass to see his work. He is eleven years old, his twelfth birthday coming soon. His favorite food is still mashed potatoes. He likes hamburgers with A-1 sauce. He hates tomatoes. He likes French toast. I would do anything for him.

The blanket rises and falls with his breathing. It is lovely to watch. Today he's going back home for his second saxophone lesson. "My teacher says I have a perfect mouth for the saxophone," he says modestly but proudly in his gentle husky little-boy voice. I love his mouth. It reminds me of bubble gum just as the sugar is released. The sun is out this morning, and it will be a warm spring day. I love him, I love the world. I can sit on the floor and touch his broad forehead, his beautiful brow. He has the intent concentrated expression of a child taking in nourishment, sleep. If I stroke his hair he might wake up, but I can't, finally, resist.

Formidable

Today my sister and I saw a cop yelling at somebody on the median at 102nd and Broadway. We could hear the commotion half a block away. What could this person have done, we wondered, to occasion so much anger. As we approached, it seemed that a man had been sleeping on the bench, and when the cop had told him to move, he had cursed. That was it. But the cop was beside himself. "Don't you ever swear at me again. Do you hear? Look at me when I'm talking to you!" By now my sister and I, both middle-aged and of some stature, we felt, and some weight, were also on the median, drawn to it by an instinct to help, to defuse the situation by our presence, by our combined years, by our formidability. The man was hunched miserably on the bench, humiliated as the cop leaned closer, still yelling. My sister and I stood there, afraid it might get worse, afraid the man was going to open his mouth and say something, get beaten up and hauled away for talking back. I remembered being a child. I remembered being a parent. Finally the cop exhausted himself. The man was ordered to get going with threats of arrest should the cop ever find him sleeping on that bench again, orders to get rid of that piece-of-shit shopping cart and all the garbage in it, threats of going downtown next time; my sister and I began to cross the street and then waited on the far curb while the man pushed his cart across. "I'm so sorry," one of us said as the man drew near. It was all we could think of. "Asshole!" he said angrily, gesturing at the cop's back. He was younger than I'd thought. Then he shrugged his shoulders and, with his voice much gentler, "Thank you," he said.

What We Want

Once in a while we have a misunderstanding, my sister and I. You are snapping at me, one of us might say. You never let me finish a sentence, the other replies. You are always criticizing me, both of us think. Recently, we hung up on each other. Then we called each other right back and found the lines busy. She's taken her phone off the hook, we both thought angrily, but anger wasn't where we wanted to wind up. Once upon a time anger was the final destination, but not now. Then my phone rang and it was my sister. Hello, we both said. I'm sorry, we both said. Then we talked about it a little. Do you still want to take a walk? she asked me. Yes, I said, and started to cry. We met at the entrance to Riverside Park at 108th, our faces blotchy and pink. This is kind of embarrassing, I said, and we both laughed. We took our walk and bought ice-cream cones and had a good time.

Because we are older now, and we know what we want.

Comfort

Before they got married her husband-to-be asked her former husband out for a cup of coffee. "I want to reassure him," he said, "that you aren't marrying a lunatic. I want him to know that the household is stable. He might worry about his daughter when she is here."

"That's a very nice idea," she said.

"How did we recognize each other?" her husband wonders now, ten years later. They are sitting at the kitchen table. "Maybe he said he would be wearing an orange hat," he says, smiling. "We were both massively indifferent to fashion." Her former husband had taken to wearing a bright orange woolen hat in cold weather. You could see him blocks away. He also had a Batman hat that one of his students had given him as a joke. And sometimes he had worn that. The orange hat kept his ears warm. Some kid had left it at his apartment. Suddenly she feels like crying. "I was probably dressed pretty much as I am now," her husband says, looking down at his flannel shirt.

"Yes," she says, "it was probably the hat."

They are trying to reconstruct the day. "It was late morning, wasn't it?" she says now.

"No, I'm sure it was night," her husband says. "I'm sure when we came out it was dark."

"I remember you didn't have a meal."

"We had cappuccino. We sat at a little table for two by the window. We were there about an hour, an hour and a half maybe. Pertutti's," he says.

"Before it moved," they say simultaneously.

"It was so nice of you," she says now, looking at his face.

"Well, it seemed the thing to do," he says modestly. "After all we did get married very quickly. He might have thought we were insane."

"Yes," she agrees. "He might have. What did you talk about?"

"We talked about you," he says. "Mostly we talked about you. And I remember thinking here we are two ordinary-looking men sitting in an ordinary restaurant having such an important conversation, just like that."

She smiles at him. "Yeah," she says, "life is amazing."

"He wanted to tell me how fragile you are," he says. "And I told him I would take good care of you."

"But I wasn't so fragile. When you got home and told me I recall being peeved." She laughs to herself.

"Well," her husband says, "you know we're all pretty fragile, really."

He is sitting opposite her. His hair has gone gray in the last ten years, but it is still wavy and, in damp weather, curly. He reminds her sometimes of a photo from the twenties, some earnest member of a college rowing team, the face you pick out from the other faces for its shining innocence and honor.

She remembers overhearing her former husband saying a year or so later that it was he who had initiated the first meeting, he who had called her husband-to-be and invited him out for coffee. She didn't say anything. He'd seemed so pleased with himself. He was getting on in years; she wanted him to be happy. She had learned by then it wasn't necessary to keep setting the record straight.

Safekeeping

My mother and father had been to Switzerland, traveling in the Engadine. When they got back, my mother told me this story. While walking in the mountains, they had come upon a small church, and a sign outside said it had been dedicated at the time of Charlemagne. She said it was the first time she'd realized there had actually been a Charlemagne, that he was not a creature of myth. It was late afternoon, getting toward dusk, and as they began to walk away, my mother said all of a sudden they could hear the disembodied voices of nuns coming through the windows of the church singing the same song they had sung at the same hour every day for the last five hundred years. "If safekeeping has a sound," she said, "then surely this was it."

My Name

You had a certain way of saying my name. It was the inflection maybe, something you put into those three syllables. And now you are gone and my name is just my name again, not the story of my life.

A Present

What is this, my sister asks again.
   It's an explanation, I answer.
   An explanation?
   It's an apology, I say.
   An apology?
   It's a present, I say.

Hugs

They were strange and unfamiliar territory and she never
knew what was expected of her inside one. What should
she be feeling? What sort of look should she wear on her
face? She was always relieved to be released from a hug
so she could move around again and assess the situation.
But now she understands. Maybe she learned from being
a grandmother. She is amazed to find (after all these
years) how simple it is. Nothing complicated is required
of you. There are no special instructions. A hug is shelter,
a dwelling place. It is dependable, durable, and easy to
assemble with what you can find at the scene of the
accident.

Look

I see the world as an extension of my mother's hand. "Look," she will say, as she has always said. And there will be a sight I might not have picked out myself, the way an old man stands at the corner, a child's shoe lost in the street, a single swan in the pond near her house. "Swans mate for life," she has probably told me a thousand times. There are things she has said I will never forget. "Look," she said once, pointing to an old wooden church at the end of a cobbled street, "it is so simple the only ornament is its own shadow."

I can read her mood by the songs she sings. Since my father died they are all love songs. She calls me because I know the words and we sing together over the phone. She has always had a lovely voice. "Just give me something to remember you by," she wanted to sing the other day. She had forgotten the chorus. "You mean after 'when you are far away from me'?" I asked. "Yes, what's that part," she said. "'Some little something that says love will not die,'" I half sing, although I know she knows these words. I can see her in my mind's eye. She is sitting in the far-left-hand corner of the big living room, where my father always sat. When he died she moved from the loveseat to his chair. Perhaps she couldn't stand to see it empty. "The Man I Love," she called later to sing. "What's the last verse?" But all I know of "The Man I Love" are the first four lines so I can't help her. She is disappointed but sings the whole song to me, minus the last bit. "Great song," I say when she is done.

It is not that we haven't had our differences. Much that I have cherished she has counted for nothing, and some of what she clings to I discount. There are times we have disappointed each other. But now she is shrinking the way old people do. She still wears stockings and shoes with little heels; I can see her in a black-and-white-print dress (too big for her now) with some sort of bow at the collar. She wears her coral necklace and her pearl necklace and a tiny round globe of a watch my father gave her that hasn't worked for years. At night she has her rituals, a chocolate on the night table in case of insomnia. Whatever book she is reading. A pillow for her little dog placed at the foot of the bed. She takes her bathrobe off (lacy and silky and slippery and blue) and lays it just so over the back of the chair. Then she puts her handbag on another smaller chair and draws it close to the bed. She sleeps on her back with her arms straight at her sides. Once she is under the covers she is so small as to almost not be there at all.

Look.

Passion

Even though she's a grandmother now she loves to watch people kiss. She loves how their arms go around each other, how their eyes close, how their lips meet. She loves watching them make out at bus stops, entrances to subway stations. Sometimes one of them is crying and she feels sad and very interested and she makes up reasons why, one or another is going away, maybe, back to Ohio or into the army. Or they are breaking up. But she likes it best when they aren't crying. Take today on the subway, for instance. She sat with a grandson on either side of her and right across was a couple eating candy out of two paper bags, feeding each other those soft pieces of yellow peanut-shaped candies and unable to keep their hands off each other. They were skinny and pale, their faces ravaged and sick, she was pretty sure they were junkies, but every time the boy leaned over to kiss the girl, the cords stood out in his neck. Oh, she thought, trembling. Such passion. Meanwhile the boys were reading a poem by a Chinese poet of the ninth century among the ads for jeans and liquor on the subway car. She smiled to herself and squeezed their warm hands because love comes and goes in so many forms and in this city passion is everywhere you look and all you have to do is breathe it in.

Ephemera

A woman and her daughter, estranged for months, come together over a box of photographs in a gallery. They look at the pictures, heads bent, hair touching, and they get lost in the images, one after another, a man's photographs of his wife and children, a backyard, domestic happiness. These are palladium prints, the color of the past, and all the more beautiful for that. They come upon the image of an enamel washbasin, in it a few cheap dishes and bowls and some debris floating in the water, silvery spoons among the dishes, as though hiding, as though about to disappear, the sun glinting off their long stems. "They look just like fish," she and her daughter exclaim together, speaking of the spoons. And then they blush, realizing what they have done.

The woman buys the photograph. It costs five hundred dollars. She knows these plates, bought for a dime, kept for a lifetime, she knows the debris in the water is berry hulls, that the children who picked the berries are just outside the kitchen door; she knows that a woman who has just dried her hands will drop the cloth on the back of a chair as a little breeze ruffles the air, and she will pause, feeling something stir inside she cannot name, and she will wait, struggling to bring it across the little bridge to consciousness, but it is already vanishing, like the red-gold spine of a fish as it dives away, she knows the woman will go outside now where her children are, supper still to come, dishes in the wash pan, a woman filled with the sensation she will one day decide to call happiness.

What I Know

It doesn't take much—the glimpse of a bare-legged girl crouching on the second-story porch of a house with five mailboxes, and I know without looking any harder that she is feeding a baby. I can see through the slats of the railing, and it is all in the curve of her back, the position of her shoulder and arm, the posture of intent. I know she is feeding a baby and the baby sits in a small plastic chair on the floor of the porch. Maybe now and then she takes a spoonful herself, if it's cereal with peaches or plum tapioca dessert in that little jar. Somewhere there are tiny shirts and crib sheets drying in the sun, and indoors a cat stretches on a beat-up chair. There is probably a sink full of dishes. Maybe she is thinking of the life she won't have now, although she loves this tiny human creature she has made out of herself. I know for years she will listen to the radio and think of boys she might have had a different future with. What is this longing, she will want to ask. This troubling feeling of more to come. *You can make something out of it,* I want to tell her. But that's what her life is for.

What the Moment Can Hold

The first time I hold my daughter's daughter I feel so sad. I don't remember feeling this when her sons were born. It is a strange feeling, the wrong emotion for this happy time, but I can't help it. I'm remembering when the baby in my arms was my daughter, when it was all still to come. So many things did not go as I would have wished. There is so much I can't undo. The baby is beautiful, as my daughter was, as all my children were and are. When I kiss my daughter she seems barely to feel it, seems almost to turn away. I wonder what she is thinking. "What a beautiful girl you have," I say, but my voice doesn't sound real. My daughter nods distractedly. I try to remember how it is when the baby is born and you are intent only on milk, milk, milk. But she feels distant to me, although I may be imagining it. This is not what I expected. I expected pure joy, and here are joy and sorrow mixing into the same moment.

Back home the family makes its adjustments, some painful. I find myself interfering, making unnecessary and unwelcome suggestions. My daughter's husband, the older boys' stepfather, asks them to do some household chore. Twice, three times, he has to ask. His voice has an edge. Everyone is tired. The older boy mutters something under his breath. Voices are raised. "You're being rude," says my daughter to her eldest son, and I jump up. I can't seem to stop myself. "He wasn't!" I shout. "You weren't listening. You're being unfair!" I am trembling with emotion. "Mother," my daughter finally has to say. "Please stop." And heartsick I leave the room. But I am remembering another family, different days. I don't know what to do with this mixture of emotions, this blurring of the present and the past, and I hate it. Instead I want one pure feeling, like water in a cup.

But the baby is beautiful. Her eyes are big and round and blue. She reminds me of one of the creatures in the Hall of Darkness, the nocturnal animals whose forms you make out only by letting your own eyes adjust, and then there they are, in the branches or among the grasses, slowly taking shape, motionless, wise, looking out at you. Beings from another world. She sleeps and wakes and nurses. She doesn't fuss. I like to carry her around the house, whispering to her, but I can't call her by her name, my name. I am humbled by the honor and don't deserve it. "What's wrong," my daughter asks from time to time. "Nothing," I say, but my heart is heavy. I feel as if my daughter and I gaze at each other on opposite banks of some body of water. "This is a happy time, Mom," she says, and I take it as a reproach.

So I cook. It comforts me to be slicing onions and frying garlic. It comforts me to be chopping tomatoes and browning meat. "You don't have to start so early, Mom," says my daughter. "It's only three o'clock, and we don't eat until seven." We laugh, but I keep on cooking. "She keeps trying to get me to eat," I hear her telling a friend on the telephone, "at ten in the morning, 'Have a chicken sandwich,' she says to me." My daughter laughs again. I look at her across the room. Her little boy is playing with trains and puzzles on the rug, occasionally climbing up next to her to look at the baby. The two older boys are in school, sixth and seventh grades. Later there will be a fire in the fireplace and a family eating supper together. I try not to think of the way she grew up, the upheavals. The ordinary things she didn't get to do, the mistakes I made.

"Do you want a pony?" I hear my daughter whisper to the baby in her arms.

At night my daughter and her husband climb the carpeted stairs to the second floor. Upstairs is another domain. This is where the smaller children sleep, and the baby, where the voices are hushed and everybody walks on tiptoe. Upstairs is dark and quiet. Downstairs the older boys and I prepare for bed, brushing our teeth, getting drinks, turning off lights. "Good night," we say to one another, and then we decide to sleep all in the same room. "It's been a long day," my oldest grandson sighs from his pile of pillows and covers on the floor. Next to me my younger grandson stretches out. I listen to them breathing until they fall asleep. Then I have a dream of a blue-black ocean where huge waves break heavy and dark. There are fangs of foam dripping from the breakers. The road home is already under swirling water, but the boys and I try to escape. It is a terrifying dream. We hang on to a rope? Each other? And I fear we will all be washed away, but then in the way of dreams suddenly the sea is calm, and the boys are with other boys, floating on their surfboards, waiting to catch a wave. The ocean is manageable again, back where it belongs. They are safe.

I lie awake, wishing I had faith of some kind. I've caught glimpses of it now and then, I can even conjure it up for a second or two, but it fades. It's a stillness, the polar opposite of worry. It isn't hope; hope has too much energy, requires constant renewal; faith (if I had it) would just be there.

The next night the baby's plastic tub is on the kitchen counter. In it a new washcloth and an unopened cake of soap, a white towel. "Are you giving her a bath tonight?" I ask, and my daughter nods. "Her first. Will you help me?" "Of course," I say, "I would love to." My daughter starts to fill the little tub with water from the sink, then stops. She decides instead that she will get into her own bathtub and take the baby in with her. I remember doing this myself a long time ago. "I'll feel more secure that way," she says. And it will feel good, warm water and the naked child against her naked self. Will I get the baby ready and bring her in? "Of course," I say. With pleasure. So I lay the baby down on my daughter's bed, and her big eyes are wide. "You are a little darling," I whisper, and bend my face to hers, but the other feeling is there too, uneasiness, something heavy in my heart. I undress her carefully, slipping one tiny arm out of its sleeve and then the other. "She's lost her umbilical cord already," I call in to my daughter. "I know, it came off early," she answers, and then I hear the water rumbling into the tub. Naked, the baby's arms and long legs flail against the bare air, and she wails. "Oh you," I whisper, unable yet to call her by my name, "it's all right." I want my joy pure, I want to get rid of the echo in my head. This is my granddaughter, named for me. This beautiful child.

I gather her up, nuzzling her soft face, and bring her into the bathroom, and my daughter, her breasts heavy with milk, reaches up her arms for the child. The moment she is lowered into the water the baby stops crying, her body goes limp, her eyelids drop—it all happens at once. Under her half-closed lids her irises are now moving left to right, over and over, rhythmically, as if to a beat. At first I am afraid, and put my hand in the water to make sure it's not too hot, but it is fine, comfortable. We don't speak, but my daughter touches my arm as we realize what we are looking at, what the two of us are being shown. This is the face of the unborn child.

And I know now what a moment can hold.

Acknowledgments

Thank you again from the bottom of my heart to Chuck Verrill, Liz Darhansoff, Leigh Feldman, and Tal Gregory, who read this at the very beginning and encouraged me and without whom I'd have just gone back to bed. Thank you to Else Blangsted, my soulmate, my friend, whose love and intelligence and refusal to take no for an answer are crucial to me. Thanks to my sisters, Judy and Eliza, who have carried me over many a rough spot and who usually make me see things more clearly and always make me laugh: I love you both. Thanks to my husband, Rich, who puts up with me with unfailing good humor and steadiness of love: How did I get so lucky? Boundless gratitude and praise for my editor, Robin Desser, who saw what this might be and made it happen, asking all the difficult interesting questions. You made the process if not pure pleasure, certainly as exhilarating as doing something difficult can get. Thank you, thank you, thank you.

As for my children, Sarah Waddell-Okin, Jennifer Waddell, Ralph Waddell, and Catherine Luttinger, what I know I've learned from all of you. I couldn't have done this (or anything) without your affection and encouragement. Thanks as well to Sarah's husband, Claude, and Ralph's wife, Kirsten. Not to mention, of course, my perfect grandchildren: Joe, Sam, Ben, Dan, Abigail, and Quinnie. (And my granddog Daisy.)

And to you, Quin, my old friend, a cup of kindness yet. Wherever you are.

Printed in the United States
by Baker & Taylor Publisher Services